Tire Pattern Image Retrieval

(轮胎花纹图像检索)

Ying Liu (刘颖)

科学出版社

北京

Responsible Editor: Wuhan Song

Copyright© 2018 by Science Press
Published by Science Press
16 Donghuangchenggen North Street
Beijing 100717, P. R. China

Printed in Beijing

All rights reserved. No part of this publication may be reproduced, stored in a retrieval system, or transmitted in any form or by any means, electronic, mechanical, photocopying, recording or otherwise, without the prior written permission of the copyright owner.

ISBN 978-7-03-059352-8

Preface

One key task in forensic science is to perform criminal investigation through image database retrieval. Of the various images, tire pattern is an important type of image data for crime scene investigation. Tire pattern image retrieval (TPIR) is an important means in providing useful clues in traffic accident control and crime case solving. However, due to the lack of standard dataset, so far there is no much work done in this field. The aim of this book is two-folded: ① To summarize the existing techniques in TPIR. ② To discuss about TPIR system design focusing on the key techniques including texture feature extraction and high-level semantic learning from tire tread pattern images.

The contribution of this book include the following: ① A comprehensive survey on the research outcome of TPIR is provided with four major categories of techniques identified including tire tread pattern retrieval, tread surface wear feature extraction, tire indentation mark retrieval and video tread pattern retrieval. ② Based on extensive experimental results on a real tire pattern database, retrieval performance of existing texture features are compared. ③ A few novel tire pattern texture feature extraction algorithms are proposed and their performance in TPIR are tested.

The proposed tire pattern texture feature extraction methods are designed based on different types of texture features with proper consideration of the inherent characteristic of tire pattern images. For example, a modified Tamura texture feature is designed for better description of tire patterns by including the global intensity information of images. A so-called H-SIFT feature is presented which intends to reduce the computational load of SIFT(scale invariant feature transform) while keeping its advantage in feature description. Two rotation-invariant texture feature extraction methods are designed making use of Radon transform, dual-tree complex wavelet transform and curvelet transform.

A very effective method named as HOG-TT is a modified version of HOG (histogram of oriented gradient) leveraging the intrinsic texture tendency (TT) of tire patterns. In addition, the application of convolutional neural network (CNN) in TPIR is discussed by explaining a transfer learning based tire pattern image feature proposed.

The content of this book is suitable for postgraduate students and researchers in the field of TPIR for literature review as well as for understanding the pros and cons of different algorithms. In addition, the book is useful for technicians in the police force as reference reading for designing practical application systems.

My gratitude to the effort from my master-degree students Zong Li, Haoyang Yan, Yuxiang Ge, Shuai Zhang in data testing, thanks also to other students Haitao Dong, Qiannan Zhang, Yanan Peng for their kind help in editing the draft.

Contents

Preface

List of Abbreviations

Chapter 1 Introduction ································· 1
   1.1 Background ······································· 1
   1.2 Contribution of This Book ························ 2
   1.3 Organization of This Book ······················· 3
   References ·· 4

Chapter 2 A Survey of Image Retrieval Techniques for Tire Pattern Database ································ 6
   2.1 Introduction ······································· 6
   2.2 Tire Pattern Database and Performance Evaluation Methods ··· 7
      2.2.1 Tire pattern image databases ·············· 8
      2.2.2 Performance evaluation ···················· 12
   2.3 Tire Pattern Retrieval ··························· 16
      2.3.1 Tire tread pattern retrieval ··············· 16
      2.3.2 Tire surface wear feature extraction ······ 21
      2.3.3 Video tire pattern retrieval ··············· 23
      2.3.4 Tire indentation mark image retrieval ···· 24
      2.3.5 Summary ·································· 27
   2.4 Discussion about Future Research Directions ····· 29
      2.4.1 Standard test dataset and performance evaluation ······ 29
      2.4.2 Matching between tire indentation mark and tire tread pattern ······································ 30

2.5 Conclusions ··· 30

References ··· 31

Chapter 3 A Modified Tamura Feature for Tire Pattern Image Description ·· 39

3.1 Introduction of Tamura Feature ······························· 39

3.2 Modification of Tamura Texture Feature ···················· 40

    3.2.1 Tamura texture feature ····································· 40

    3.2.2 Modification ·· 44

3.3 Experimental Results ··· 47

3.4 Conclusions ·· 49

References ··· 49

Chapter 4 H-SIFT: SIFT from High-Frequency Information of Tire Pattern Images ·············· 51

4.1 Introduction of SIFT Feature ··································· 51

4.2 Review of SIFT Feature ·· 52

    4.2.1 Scale space and relevant concepts ······················· 53

    4.2.2 The model of Gaussian pyramid and difference of Gaussian pyramid ··· 55

    4.2.3 The establishment of the key points ···················· 57

    4.2.4 The key points matching ·································· 59

4.3 Description of the Proposed Method H-SIFT ·············· 60

4.4 Experimental Results ··· 62

4.5 Conclusions ·· 64

References ··· 64

Chapter 5 Study on Rotation-Invariant Texture Feature Extraction for Tire Pattern Retrieval ·········· 66

5.1 Introduction ··· 66

5.2 Radon-DTCWT Algorithm ······································ 68

Contents   v

        5.2.1   Radon transform ································· 68

        5.2.2   Translation sensitivity of ridgelet transform ············ 69

        5.2.3   The new Radon-DTCWT algorithm ··················· 72

   5.3   Curvelet Energy Distribution Algorithm ····················· 75

        5.3.1   Curvelet transform of tire pattern image ················ 75

        5.3.2   Direction characteristics of tire pattern images ·········· 76

        5.3.3   Implementation of curvelet energy distribution

                algorithm ···································· 78

   5.4   Experiment Results ································· 80

   5.5   Conclusions ······································· 83

References ··· 83

Chapter 6   HOG-TT: A Robust HOG-Based Texture Feature Extraction Method Making Use of Texture Tendency in Tread Pattern Images ···· 86

   6.1   Introduction ······································· 86

   6.2   Description of HOG-TT ······························ 88

        6.2.1   HOG descriptor ································ 88

        6.2.2   HOG-TT ····································· 89

   6.3   Experimental Results ································ 93

   6.4   Conclusions ······································· 97

References ··· 97

Chapter 7   FF-TL: An Effective Tread Pattern Image Classification Algorithm Based on Transfer Learning ···································· 99

   7.1   Introduction ······································· 99

   7.2   Related Work ····································· 101

        7.2.1   Convolutional neural network ······················ 101

        7.2.2   Transfer learning ······························· 102

7.3 Proposed Algorithm · 103
7.3.1 Fine-tuning the network · 104
7.3.2 Feature extraction, feature fusion and SVM classification · 104
7.4 Experimental Results · 105
7.4.1 Experimental dataset and performance evaluation parameter · 105
7.4.2 Experimental results and analysis · 106
7.5 Conclusions · 108
References · 109

Chapter 8 Summary and Future Work · 113
8.1 Summary of the Book · 113
8.2 Discussion of Future Work · 115
8.3 Acknowledgment · 116

Appendix 1: CIIP Tread Indentation Database · · · · · · · · · · · · · · 117
Appendix 2: CIIP Tread Pattern Database · · · · · · · · · · · · · · · · · · 118

List of Abbreviations

crime scene investigation(CSI)

crime scene investigation image retrieval (CSIR)

content-based image retrieval (CBIR)

tire pattern image retrieval (TPIR)

tread pattern image dataset (TPID)

convolutional neural network (CNN)

Center for Image and Information Processing(CIIP)

receiver operating characteristic (ROC)

false accept rate (FAR)

false rejection rate (FRR)

equivalence error rate (EER)

precision-recall curve (PRC)

precision-recall ratio(PVR)

scale-invariant feature transform (SIFT)

discrete wavelet transform (DWT)

dual tree complex wavelet transform (DT-CWT)

curvelet energy distribution (CED)

principal component analysis (PCA)

support vector machine (SVM)

curvelet energy distribution algorithm(CEDA)

hierarchical fuzzy pattern matching classifier (HFPMC)

fuzzy c-means clustering (FCM)

mutual information (MI)

dependent component analysis (DCA)

List of Abbreviations

Fourier transformation (FT)

texture tendency (TT)

histogram of oriented gradient (HOG)

cell feature vector (CFV)

global feature vector (GFV)

classification accuracy (CA)

algorithm running time (ART)

curvelet domain energy distribution algorithm (CEDA)

compressed histogram of oriented gradients (CHOG)

gray level co-occurrence matrix (GLCM)

dual path networks (DPN)

transfer learning (TL)

Chapter 1

Introduction

1.1 Background

Crime scene investigation (CSI) images are generally collected by crime detectives at crime scene, which are closely related to the crime and have become an important part of on-the-spot investigative information. Crime scene investigation image retrieval (CSIR) can provide vital clues for uncovering of the crime and it plays a vital role in solving serial crimes [1]. With the wide use of the camera equipments and the continued increase of CSI images, effective and efficient CSIR becomes more and more important to improve the work of the crime investigation and greatly save the human resources[2-6].

Content-based image retrieval (CBIR) is used to extract the low-level visual feature from the raw image and then integrates them to high-level semantic feature to provide a meaningful representation of image content. A distance metric between feature vectors is used to measure the image similarity and it can subsequently be used to conduct the image database retrieval[7,8]. The key phases in CBIR include the low-level visual feature extraction, image similarity measuring and high-level semantic feature extraction[6]. Although image retrieval techniques have been developed for many years, little attention by far has been paid to the CSIR due to the lack of available image data samples. Due to the different characteristics of CSI images, the CBIR algorithms developed for general images are not always suitable for CSIR[9].

Of the various CSI images, tire pattern is an important type of image data for crime scene investigation. Tire pattern image retrieval (TPIR) is an important means in providing useful clues in traffic accident control and crime case solving. Due to the lack of standard test bed in this area, the research work in this area is not that rich, though much has been done in CBIR on general images.

1.2 Contribution of This Book

The aim of this book is to discuss about TPIR focusing on the key techniques such as effective texture feature extraction and high-level semantic learning from tire tread pattern images. The contribution of this book include mainly the following.

First, a comprehensive survey on the research outcome of this area is provided including available datasets and performance evaluation criteria. In addition, four major categories of techniques in tire pattern image retrieval are identified including tire tread pattern retrieval, tread surface wear feature extraction, tire indentation mark retrieval and video tread pattern retrieval. For each category, state-of-the-art techniques on low-level texture feature extraction and high-level semantic learning are described.

Secondly, based on extensive experimental results on a real tire pattern database, performance comparison of existing texture features on description of tire pattern images is presented, which helps to explain the special characteristic of tire pattern images.

Thirdly, a few novel tire pattern texture feature extraction algorithms are presented in details.

(1) A modified Tamura texture feature which improves the performance of Tamura feature by including global intensity of images.

(2) Using DWT to obtain the high-frequency information of tire pattern image (so called H-image) and then obtain SIFT feature of the H-image as H-SIFT. Thus, the computational load of SIFT is greatly reduced with reasonable lost in retrieval performance.

(3) Three different robust texture feature extraction methods based on Radon transform and dual-tree complex wavelet transform, curvelet transform and histogram of oriented gradient(HOG).

(4) The performance of convolutional neural network(CNN) on TPIR based on transfer learning.

1.3 Organization of This Book

Chapter 2 gives an intensive survey in the area of TPIR, focusing on describing texture feature extraction and high-level semantic learning methods for tire pattern images. In addition. the tire tread pattern image database available and the performance evaluation parameters used in literature. Chapter 3 introduces a modified Tamura texture feature designed for better description of tire pattern images by including the global intensity information of images. Based on the observation that tire pattern image contains rich high-frequency information. Chapter 4 presents a H-SIFT method which reduces the computational cost of traditional SIFT by focusing only on the high-frequency information of the image. Two rotation-invariant texture feature extraction methods are presented in Chapter 5 making use of Radon transform, dual-tree complex wavelet transform, and curvelet transform. The method described in Chapter 6 is named as HOG-TT which is a modified version of HOG (histogram of oriented gradient) leveraging the intrinsic texture tendency (TT) of tire patterns. In Chapter 7, the application of convolutional neural network (CNN) in TPIR is discussed by explaining a transfer learning based tire pattern image feature proposed. Chapter 8 concludes the book with a few potential future research directions suggested.

References

[1] HAN N, CHEN W. Research on serial case based on cluster analysis[J]. Journal of Chinese People's Public Security University (Science and technology), 2012, 18(1): 53-58.

[2] LIU Y, ZHANG D, LIU G. A survey of content-based image retrieval with high-level semantics[J]. Pattern recognition, netherlands, 2007, 40(1): 262-282.

[3] LIU Y. Semantic-Based Image Retrieval [M]. Beijing: Science Press, 2016.

[4] ARYAL S, KAI M T, HAFFARI G, et al. Beyond tf-idf and Cosine Distance in Documents Dissimilarity Measure[C]//Brisbane: Asia Information Retrieval Symposium, Springer International Publishing, 2015: 400-406.

[5] SU J H, HUANG W J, YU P S, et al. Efficient relevance feedback for content-based image retrieval by mining user navigation patterns[J]. IEEE transactions on knowledge & data engineering archive, 2011, 23(3): 360-372.

[6] CHEN Y, WANG J Z. A region-based fuzzy feature matching approach to content-based image retrieval[J]. IEEE transactions on pattern analysis

& machine intelligence, USA, 2002, 24(9): 1252-1267.

[7] XU S P, LI C Q, JIANG S L, et al. Similarity measures for content-based image retrieval based on intuitionistic fuzzy set theory[J]. Journal of computers, 2012, 7(7): 1733-1742.

[8] DENG J, SOCHER R, Li F F, et al. ImageNet: A large-scale hierarchical image database[C]. IEEE Conference on Computer Vision and Pattern Recognition, Miami, 2009: 248-255.

[9] LIU Y, HUANG Y, GAO Z. Feature extraction and similarity measure for crime scene investigation image retrieval[J]. Journal of Xi'an University of Posts and Telecommunications, 2014, 19(6): 11-16.

Chapter 2

A Survey of Image Retrieval Techniques for Tire Pattern Database

2.1 Introduction

A tire pattern is regarded as a fingerprint of a vehicle. Just like fingerprints are used to identify a person in many important applications, tire patterns also play a critical role in vehicle identification. For example, tire tread patterns are important clues in police case solving and traffic accident management[1]. In business world, tire pattern design patent is a major cause of commercial disputes in tire industry[2]. Hence, it is necessary to design effective and efficient tire pattern retrieval systems.

Tire pattern image is rich in texture with clear edges, and tire patterns of same model have similar textures[3]. Although content-based image retrieval (CBIR) has been studied for decades[4], little has been done for tire pattern retrieval, due to the scarcity of test datasets. This chapter provides a comprehensive survey of the research achievement in the field of tire pattern image database retrieval. Tire pattern datasets and performance evaluation parameters are first described.

2.2 Tire Pattern Database and Performance Evaluation Methods

Then, according to the application scenarios (such as tire pattern patent protection, tire source tracking, vehicle tire identification, etc.), existing techniques in tire pattern retrieval are classified into four categories, including tire tread pattern retrieval, tread surface wear feature extraction, video tread pattern retrieval and tire indentation mark retrieval. Finally, based on the survey and the demand from real-world applications, research challenges in this area are discussed and a few promising future research directions are suggested.

In this chapter, Section 2.2 introduces different tire pattern datasets available, and the measurements used to evaluate the performance of tire pattern retrieval. In Section 2.3, four categories of tire pattern retrieval techniques are identified according to the application scenarios. Section 2.4 suggests a few future research directions. Finally, Section 2.5 concludes the chapter.

2.2 Tire Pattern Database and Performance Evaluation Methods

Literature survey shows that there are a number of research groups working in this area, including Matej Bel University of Slovenia[4], Michigan University[5], University of Maryland[6], Korea University[7], Palo Alto Research Center in USA[8], Center for Image and Information Processing(CIIP) of Xi'an University of Posts and Telecommunications (XUPT)[9-13], Shaanxi Normal University[14-20], Jilin University in China[21-33], Dalian Maritime University in China[34], Beijing Jiaotong University[35-37], etc.

This section introduces tire pattern datasets and retrieval performance evaluation measurements used in literature.

2.2.1 Tire pattern image databases

There is no standard dataset for test in this field so far, and researchers have to collect and create their own data sets. There are four types of tire pattern image data including tire tread pattern (fraction of a tire showing texture pattern of a tire surface), tire indentation mark (mark left by a tire on the ground), tire surface wear (fraction of tire showing the wear of a tire), and video tire pattern (tire pattern image in video sequence), examples are given in Fig.2-1. Table 2-1 lists some of the datasets in literature with examples given in Fig.2-2.

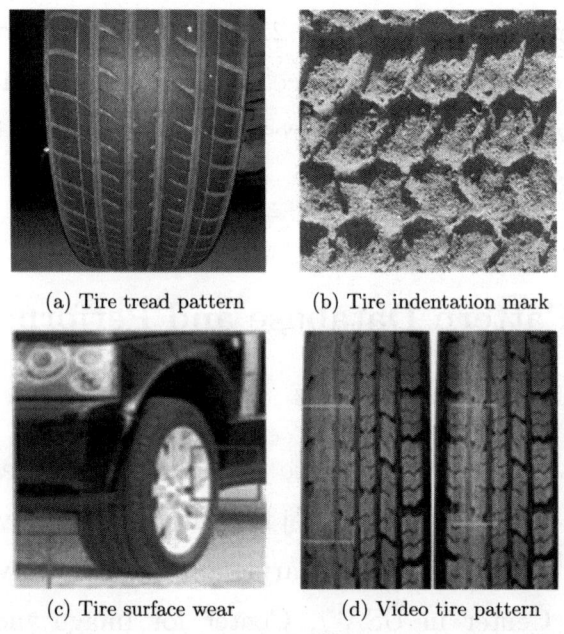

(a) Tire tread pattern   (b) Tire indentation mark

(c) Tire surface wear   (d) Video tire pattern

Fig. 2-1   Four different types of tire pattern images

A tire tread pattern is the textural or structural pattern of a tire. Tire tread images usually capture the original local structures of a tire surface with high resolution and such data can be used for tire pattern classification and retrieval[1,9,13]. A tire surface wear is a patch of

2.2 Tire Pattern Database and Performance Evaluation Methods

Table 2-1　Tire pattern datasets available in literature

Database and Organization	Amount of Data
Tire pattern patent database Qingdao Rubber Valley Enterprise, China	520,000 tire tread patterns
CIIP tire pattern database CIIP of XUPT, China http://user.qzone.qq.com/3225702926/2	5,100 tread patterns/102 classes; 1,000 tire indentation marks/200 classes
Tire indentation mark dataset Dalian Maritime University, China	2,976 images of 496 classes
Tire surface wear dataset University of Maryland, USA	1,320 tire surface wear
Tire tread pattern and video snapshot www.tirerack.com TIRE RACK in USA	5,530 tire tread patterns /274 videos
Tire tread pattern dataset Shaanxi Normal University, China	210 images in 7 classes
VisualFoxPro: Tire indentation mark dataset, including tire model, product date, etc., Jilin University, China	About 10,000 records of data

diminished or disappearing tire pattern, and it is a contrast with the background tire tread pattern. Relevant research work focuses on studying the characteristics of tire surface wear for tire identification[36,37]. A tire indentation is a tire print on ground. Due to the tire deformation, a tire indentation on ground is usually a distorted or broken tire tread pattern. In addition, tire indentation mark is susceptible to the change of the carrier and same tire pattern might appear very different on different carriers. Relevant research work focuses mainly on tire indentation mark enhancement and recognition[21-34]. A video tire pattern captures a remote view of a tire. It is usually a low resolution image or a silhouette of a tire pattern. A low resolution tire tread pattern from side view can usually be obtained from a tire video. Textures in such images are often incomplete or even distorted, due to motion blur or the angle at which the video is taken. These data are analyzed for classification of different types of tires such as snow tire, rain tire, etc.[38]

There are several large datasets available from the industry. For example, Qingdao Rubbber Vally Enterprise has a database with about 520,000 tire patterns of different types[2], examples are given in Fig. 2-2(a). However, such datasets are usually not open to researchers due to patent protection.

Most tire tread pattern datasets created by researcher groups are of smaller scale compared to the industrial datasets, and the largest available so far belongs to CIIP of XUPT in China, which contains 5,100 tire tread pattern images of different models [39], examples are given in Fig.2-2(b). Tire indentation marks are not easy to obtain. Fig.2-2(c) provides examples from CIIP database. Dalian Maritime University in China has a tire indentation mark dataset containing 2,976 images in 496 classes of which 16 classes are low quality images taken at traffic accident scene[34]. Examples of this dataset are provided in Fig.2-2(d).

Colbry et al.[6] from University of Maryland in USA build a tire surface wear dataset with 1,320 images, as shown in Fig.2-2(e). Tire pattern images from surveillance video are usually of lower resolution compared with other types of tire pattern images. The dataset from TIRE RACK[40] contains 5,530 tire tread patterns and 274 videos. Samples of video tire pattern images are given in Fig.2-2(f). Fig.2-2(g) shows tread pattern examples from TIRE RACK database. The database records also other information such as the brand of vehicle, model of tire, etc. Fig.2-2(h) provides examples of tire tread patterns from Shaanxi Nor-

2.2 Tire Pattern Database and Performance Evaluation Methods 11

mal University in China, and Fig.2-2(i) displays tire indentation marks from the dataset of Jilin University in China.

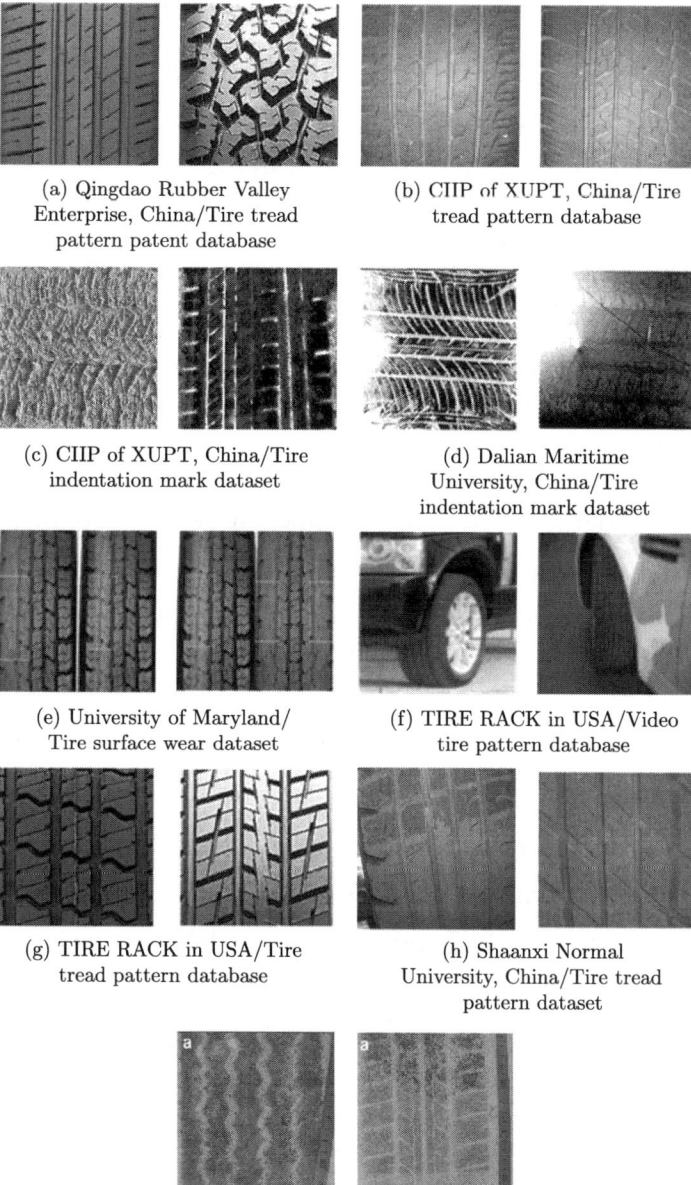

(a) Qingdao Rubber Valley Enterprise, China/Tire tread pattern patent database

(b) CIIP of XUPT, China/Tire tread pattern database

(c) CIIP of XUPT, China/Tire indentation mark dataset

(d) Dalian Maritime University, China/Tire indentation mark dataset

(e) University of Maryland/Tire surface wear dataset

(f) TIRE RACK in USA/Video tire pattern database

(g) TIRE RACK in USA/Tire tread pattern database

(h) Shaanxi Normal University, China/Tire tread pattern dataset

(i) Jilin University, China/Tire indentation mark dataset

Fig.2-2 Examples of tire pattern datasets

2.2.2 Performance evaluation

Most CBIR systems so far emphasize retrieval precision only, that is, effectiveness of the algorithm. In [41], however, the author elaborates performance evaluation in three aspects reflecting the effectiveness (retrieval precision), efficiency (retrieval speed) and flexibility (adaptability to different application scenarios) of a system.

As there is no standard performance evaluation mechanism yet, it is difficult for researchers to compare their experimental results. For different applications such as tire pattern recognition, tire pattern retrieval, tire surface wear feature extraction, different performance measurements have been used.

Recognition rate is commonly used to evaluate the effectiveness of tire pattern recognition[17]. As in equation (2-1), recognition rate is defined as the amount of correct recognition (n) over the total number of images tested (N), which explains the classification performance of an algorithm.

$$R = \left(\frac{n}{N}\right) \times 100\% \qquad (2\text{-}1)$$

Several other measurements have also been used in literature to evaluate the performance of tire pattern image retrieval, such as the matching time, number of matching pairs, false accept rate (FAR), false rejection rate (FRR), equivalence error rate (EER), receiver operating characteristic (ROC) curve.

Matching time is the amount of time taken in finding the match for the query image from the database. Number of matching pairs refers to the amount of matching pairs within the distance threshold between their features vectors[42]. The FRR and FAR are defined as following[42],

$$\text{FRR} = \left(\frac{\text{NFR}}{\text{NGRA}}\right) \times 100\% \qquad (2\text{-}2)$$

2.2 Tire Pattern Database and Performance Evaluation Methods

$$\text{FAR} = \left(\frac{\text{NFA}}{\text{NIRA}}\right) \times 100\% \qquad (2\text{-}3)$$

where NGRA is the number of within-class tests performed, NIRA is the number of between-class tests performed. NFR and NFA refer to the amount of false rejection and false accept, respectively [43]. The equivalence error rate (EER) is defined as the probability that NFR equals to NFA. By plotting both FAR and FRR on the same graph, the ROC curve is obtained as shown in Fig.2-3. Draw the line $y = x$ as the dash line in Fig.2-3, the intersection of this line with the ROC curve has its x-coordinate or y-coordinate as the EER[43], which corresponds to the highest recognition rate.

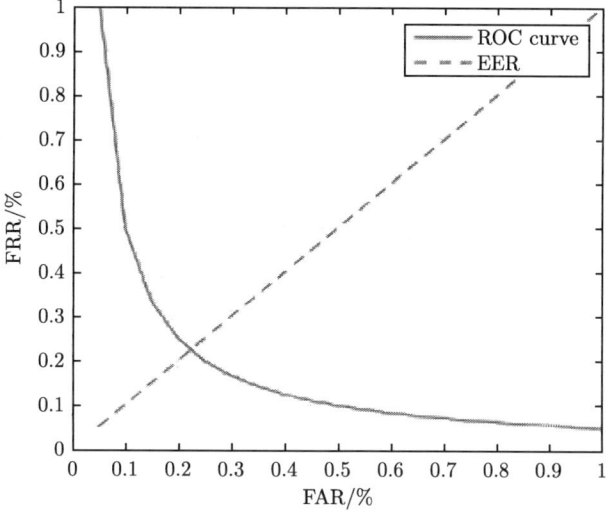

Fig.2-3 An example of receiver operating characteristic (ROC) curve

Classification accuracy (or classification rate) and mutual information are also often used for tire pattern classification performance evaluation. As shown in equation (2-4), classification accuracy (Q) is the number of correctly classified images (N) over the total amount of images tested (M).

$$Q = \left(\frac{N}{M}\right) \times 100\% \qquad (2\text{-}4)$$

The mutual information between sample X and sample Y is defined as:

$$I(X,Y) = H(X) + H(Y) - H(X,Y) \qquad (2\text{-}5)$$

where $H(X,Y)$ is the joint entropy:

$$H(X,Y) = -\sum P(x,y)\mathrm{lb}(x,y) \qquad (2\text{-}6)$$

where $P(x,y)$ is the joint-probability.

In [41] and [43], precision (P), recall (R) and precision-recall curve (PRC), precision-recall ratio (PVR), are used to measure the effectiveness of tire pattern retrieval. Precision and recall tells the ratio of correct-retrieval over the total number of image returned, and the total number of images in the database, respectively.

The formulas define the precision and recall are shown in the following, where A is the set of relevant images, B is the set of retrieved images.

$$P = p(A|B) = \frac{p(A \cup B)}{p(B)} \qquad (2\text{-}7)$$

$$R = p(B|A) = \frac{p(A \cup B)}{p(A)} \qquad (2\text{-}8)$$

The precision curve takes precision as the y-coordinate and the total number of image returned as the x-coordinate. PVR curve[41] is obtained with recall as the x-axis and precision as y-axis in Fig.2-4.

PVR ratio $S_f^{[41]}$ is obtained by computing the area under the PVR curve. The larger the PVR ratio is, the better the retrieval performance.

$$S_f = \int f(x,y)\mathrm{d}x \qquad (2\text{-}9)$$

2.2 Tire Pattern Database and Performance Evaluation Methods

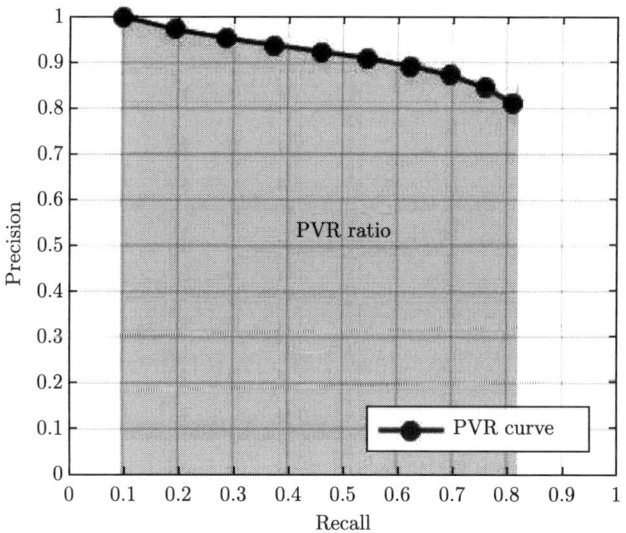

Fig.2-4 PVR curve and PVR ratio

The authors in [34] use Mean Sort for retrieval performance evaluation, which refers to the mean ranking order of the correct-matches among all the images returned. This measurement effectively describes the ordering of the retrieval results. Suppose N is the total number of images retrieved, among the N retrieved images, there are N_R relevant to the query, d_r is the corresponding rank of an image, $\hat{N}_R$ is the total amount of relevant images in the database, the Mean Sort is calculated as:

$$K = \frac{1}{N\hat{N}_R} \left[\sum_{r=1}^{\hat{N}_R} d_r - \frac{\hat{N}_R(\hat{N}_R - 1)}{2} \right] \qquad (2\text{-}10)$$

Jung et al.[8] proposed Clustering Validity as performance measurement for clustering, which tells whether all samples belong to same cluster. The process to measure clustering performance is called clustering validity analysis. Clustering optimization is to minimize within-class distance and maximize between-class distance. The closer the clustering is to the optimized clustering, the better the performance. Whether all samples belong to same cluster, that is to say, whether the clustered samples all belong to the cluster it should be in and whether there are errors in clustering results.

2.3 Tire Pattern Retrieval

This section reviews four categories of existing tire pattern retrieval techniques including: ① tire tread pattern retrieval, ② tire surface wear feature extraction, ③ video tire pattern retrieval, and ④ tire indentation mark retrieval. For each category, low-level texture extraction and high-level semantic learning techniques are described in details.

2.3.1 Tire tread pattern retrieval

Compared with other three types of tire patterns, texture in tire tread pattern image is clearer and has more details. More work has been done processing this type of data than research work on the other three types of data.

1. Low-level texture feature

1) Spatial domain texture feature
Because tire tread patterns have rich textures such as edges and structures, there are a number of works have used improved versions of traditional texture extraction algorithms to describe the texture features of tire patterns, such as Tamura texture feature[10,44], SIFT (scale invariant feature transform)[12], gray-level co-occurrence matrix (GLCM)[45].

Tamura texture suite contains six features: coarseness, contrast, directionality, linearity, regularity and roughness, and the first three are usually used for image retrieval. Hao et al.[46] proposed a variant of

2.3 Tire Pattern Retrieval

Tamura texture feature. They used histogram of coarseness and histogram of edge angles to replace coarseness and contrast in the Tamura texture suite. Experimental results demonstrated improvement in retrieval precision compared with Tamura feature.

The contrast in Tamura feature describes the global distribution of image intensity, but does not describe well the local feature of texture. Liu et al.[10] proposed to use the statistics obtained from the histogram of intensity to provide local information of texture description, including mean, standard deviation, smoothness, third moment, consistency and entropy. Experimental results on tire pattern database showed the effectiveness of the proposed algorithm outperforms the method in [46].

2) Frequency domain texture feature

Frequency domain texture features of tire tread patterns are usually obtained by calculating the statistics of transform domain coefficients using two-dimensional fast fourier transforms (2D-FFT)[47], Radon transform[48], dual tree complex wavelet transform (DT-CWT)[49-51], curvelet transform[52-54], discrete wavelet transform (DWT)[55], etc.

As DWT-based texture feature is sensitive to image rotation and is not translation-invariant, it is less robust for tire pattern texture feature description[56]. To overcome the disadvantages of DWT, dual tree complex wavelet transform (DT-CWT) was proposed by Selesnick et al.[57] in 2005. DT-CWT not only is good at capturing local changes in spatial domain, but also has shift invariant (or translation invariant) property and less data redundancy. In [11], Yan et al. presented a texture feature extraction method based on both Radon transform and DT-CWT, which made use of the rotation-invariant property of Radon transform and the translation-invariant property of DT-CWT to provide rotation and translation-invariant texture features. This method first applies Radon transform on an image and then performs DT-CWT on the coefficients in Radon domain. The mean and variance of the coefficients in each subband in DT-CWT domain are concatenated as the texture feature vector. Experimental results from a set of 200 tire pattern images of 40 classes show that the proposed method outperforms the DWT based method.

In [56], Liu et al. proposed a texture feature extraction method for tire tread pattern based on curvelet energy distribution (CED). It is observed that there are mainly four types of tire tread patterns according to the directions of tire textures: vertical, horizontal, diagonal, and mixed. Examples are displayed in Fig.2-5.

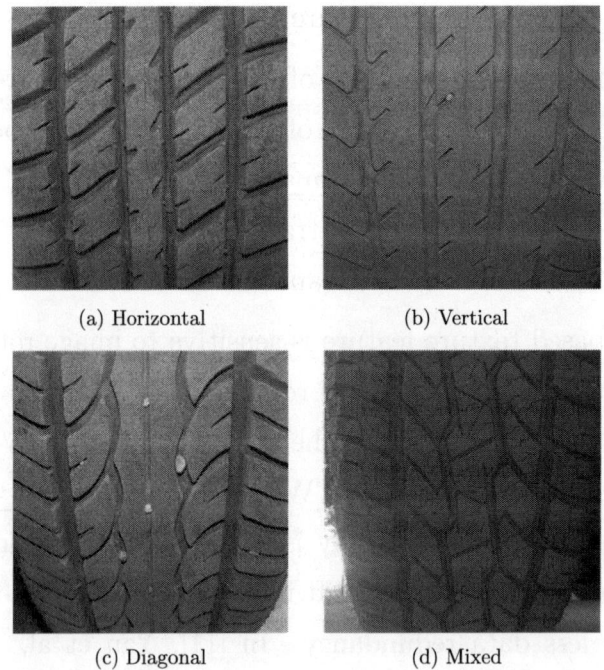

Fig.2-5 Four types of tire tread patterns

The authors found that the direction of tire pattern texture is related to the energy distribution in curvelet domain, and the main direction

2.3 Tire Pattern Retrieval

corresponds to the subband with highest energy proportion. Based on this observation, a CED-based texture feature was proposed with the following procedure: ① Perform 2-level curvelet transform on a tire pattern, and obtain 13 subbands as shown in Fig.2-6(b). ② Mean and variance of the real and imaginary parts of each subbands are calculated and form a texture feature of 52 dimensions, in the order as shown in Fig. 2-6(c): level 2 subbands in S_3 followed by level 1 subbands in S_2 followed by level 0 subbands S_1. ③ Shift the 52-D feature vector obtained in step ② until the subband with largest energy proportion takes the first place in S_2 and S_3. ④ The resulted feature vector is used as the texture descriptor of the tire pattern.

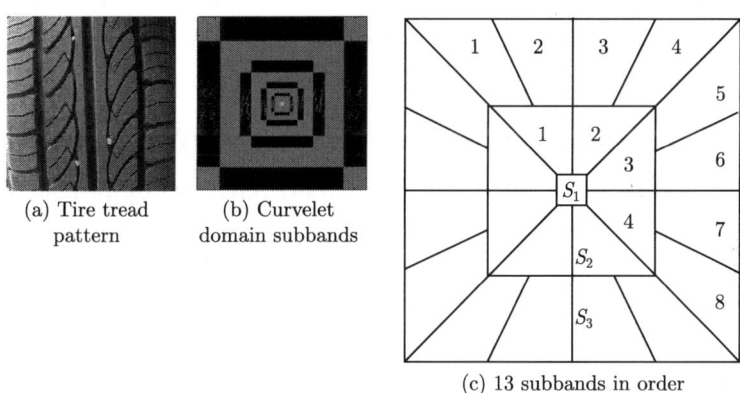

(a) Tire tread pattern (b) Curvelet domain subbands (c) 13 subbands in order

Fig.2-6 Curvelet transform

Using the same dataset of 200 tire tread pattern as in [11], the proposed texture feature is shown to be rotation and translation invariant and improves not only the effectiveness (retrieval precision), but also the efficiency (time) of tire pattern retrieval.

3) Fusion of spatial and frequency-domain features

Jia et al.[45] presented a texture feature extraction method combining DWT and GLCM, which takes the advantage of both DWT and GLCM to capture both spectral and special features of a tire pattern. Experimental results show that the proposed method outperformed either DWT or GLCM for tire pattern retrieval.

SIFT feature is known to provide high retrieval accuracy for tire pattern retrieval, but its computation is very high because of the large amount of feature points to be calculated, and thus it is not suitable for real-time implementation. In [12], Wang et al. designed an algorithm which combines DWT and SIFT in a way that the high-frequency sub-bands in DWT domain are used to obtain a so called H-image which contains most of the texture information of the tire pattern, then SIFT is applied on the H-image instead of the original image. The purpose is to preserve the texture information of the tire pattern (texture details corresponds to high-frequency coefficients in DWT domain) with less amount of SIFT feature points by discarding the low-frequency information of the image. In their experiments, 2-level DWT was applied. Experimental results on a set of 200 tire tread patterns demonstrated that on average, the amount of feature points is reduced by about 71.25% with slight drop in retrieval accuracy.

2. High-level semantic learning

Machine learning techniques such as principal component analysis (PCA)[5] and support vector machine (SVM)[58] are used to convert low-level texture features of tire pattern to high-level semantics which is the name of the 15 types of tire patterns. In [8], Jung et al. proposed a hierarchical fuzzy pattern matching classifier (HFPMC) for tire pattern recognition. In this method, fuzzy c-means clustering (FCM) is first used to create a Binary Decision Tree. At each node of the tree, based on clustering validity (which tells whether all samples belong to a same cluster), a subset of feature points which best split the labelled

2.3 Tire Pattern Retrieval

data into two dissimilar groups are selected. Next, the subset of selected feature points is used to reconstruct the hierarchical clustering structure. At every level of the hierarchy, the corresponding cluster center is used to define the reference fuzzy sets and prototypes for the HFPMC. Experimental results show that HFPMC has reasonable effectiveness on tire tread pattern classification. However, the complexity of the method limits its application in practical scenarios.

Yuan, Chin and Wei from Dayeh University, presented a tire tread pattern recognition method based on Gabor transform and SVM [58]. They first enhances tire pattern image using morphological processing, Gabor transform is then applied to obtain frequency coefficients and texture features are finally obtained using PCA analysis. The resulted features are used to train the SVM for classification purpose. Experimental results from a dataset of 90 tire patterns of 15 classes show that the method achieves a recognition rate up to 60.0%.

Guo et al. proposed a multi-feature and multi-level SVM mechanism for tire pattern retrieval. The multiple types of texture features include the variance of each subband from the contourlet transform domain, and other statistics such as secondary moment, entropy and contrast computed from the GLCM. At classification stage, a decision tree based SVM is trained for classification task. Experimental results from a database of 210 tire tread patterns with 7 classes show that the average recognition rate is up to 99.5%.

2.3.2 Tire surface wear feature extraction

For reasons such as road conditions, it is natural that tire pattern will produce specific surface wear. It is found that surface wear on tires of same model tend to show similar pattern. Hence, such features can be used to distinguish between different types of tire patterns. This section introduces tire surface wear feature extraction including low-level texture feature and high-level semantic derivation.

1. Low-level texture feature

1) Spatial domain features

In [35], [37] and [39], gray-level thresholding-based segmentation method (Ostu's threshold selection method) is used to obtain spatial domain tire surface wear features. In the gray-level thresholding image segmentation, in order to properly separate foreground from an image, the key is to choose a suitable threshold. Basically, the Ostu algorithm assumes that the image contains two classes of pixels: foreground pixels and background pixels, it then calculates the optimum threshold separating the two classes so that their combined spread (intra-class variance) is minimal. The segmentation performance is good when the contrast between the background and the target area in the foreground is high.

To describe the characteristics of tire surface wear, centroid, area, perimeter, and intensity (the proportions of different gray-levels in the region) of a region are defined[36]. With thresholding scheme, these parameters can be used to distinguish between worn and not-worn region.

2) Frequency domain texture feature

Zhang et al.[36] proposed a tire surface wear detection method using DWT and thresholding-based template matching technique. Features such as centroid, area, perimeter and intensity distribution in the region are obtained to describe the degree of surface wear. By comparing the feature with the threshold which is defined based on surface wear features [33], a tire region can be identified as worn or not.

2.3 Tire Pattern Retrieval

2. High-level semantics learning

In [7], Wei et al. presented an adaptive co-training mechanism based on mutual information (MI) for tire surface wear segmentation. Co-training is a powerful semi-supervised machine learning method which can achieve high classification accuracy even on a training data set with only a small set of labeled data. The performance of co-training relies on the diversity and sufficiency of the features. The authors described a novel mutual information based approach based on dependent component analysis (DCA) in order to achieve feature splits that are maximally independent between-subsets (diversity) or within-subsets (sufficiency). Experimental results on a tire tread pattern database of 1,320 images show that the proposed approach achieves higher accuracy than supervised classification.

2.3.3 Video tire pattern retrieval

Compared with tire patterns taken as still image, video tire pattern images suffer from variety in camera angle, incomplete tire pattern, low resolution and dynamic blurring[38]. Fig.2-2(f) shows two examples.

Bulan et al.[38] proposed a video tire pattern classification algorithm by combining principal component analysis (PCA) and support vector machine (SVM). This algorithm is used for classification of both video tire patterns (often with dynamic blurring) and still tire patterns. For feature extraction, PCA is used to obtain low-dimensional feature of the tire surface from its binary contour, SVM is then applied for classification purpose.

Based on a dataset of 347 still images (40 taken in snow, 70 taken in all-seasons, 70 taken in summer and 167 images taken in complex environment). The classification accuracy for each class is 97.86%, 84.79%,

93.36% and 87.43%, respectively. For video tire pattern testing, with six snow videos and five all-season videos, the classification accuracy is up to 81.81%.

2.3.4 Tire indentation mark image retrieval

The feature of tire indentation mark image varies with the different indentation carriers (such as land, snow), therefore, the indentation pattern is different from the original tire pattern. Texture information of tire indentation mark image is more susceptible to illumination, indentation carriers and image shooting angle. These images often suffer from texture broken, deformation, blur, noise and other problems. Hence, image pre-processing and enhancement are important for tire indentation mark retrieval[18]. This section describes existing techniques in this area.

1. Low-level texture feature

1) Spatial-domain texture feature
Spatial methods of tire indentation feature extraction include edge detection (sobel, roberts, log, canny), color space transform (RGB, HSV, NTSC)[24], CV model (Chan-Vese active contour model)[31] and SIFT[33].

CV model is smoothing, anti-noise and topological variable. It is suitable for processing tire indentation mark images which have more edges and more branches. In [31], the CV model is used for extracting the edge information of the tire indentation mark, and the SIFT feature is then computed and used for matching purpose. Experimental results on a dataset of tire indentation mark images with noise, stretching, rotation, color cast, fuzzy change, their average recognition rate is up to 80%.

2.3 Tire Pattern Retrieval

The method in [24] first converts RGB color space of an image to HSV and NTSC space, and extracts image edge information based on chromatic aberration which basically separates an image signal into three color channels. Chromatic aberration, also called chromatic distortion, and spherochromatism, is a dispersion phenomenon in optic due to the lens' failure in focusing all colors to the same convergence point[60]. Chromatic aberration manifests itself as "fringes" of color along boundaries that separate dark and bright parts of the image, because different colors in the optical spectrum cannot be focused to a single common point[61]. Canny operator is then applied to produce the edge images with clear texture patterns. Such edge information of tire indentation mark is proved to be useful for retrieval purpose. Tire indentation mark image is susceptible to the change of the carrier, therefore the background of the image is usually varied, and the indentation mark pattern is usually incomplete, deformed and fuzzy. With the combination of the CV model and SIFT method, the indentation marks can be well represented, thereby reducing the influence of the carrier on the tire indentation mark pattern information.

2) Frequency-domain texture feature

To extract tire indentation feature in frequency domain, transformations such as Fourier transformation (FT)[62,63], Gabor transform[21,28] are used to convert the image into frequency domain. Wang[21] described a method combining Gabor transform and SIFT to reduce the computation cost of SIFT. At feature matching stage of SIFT, Gabor transform is used for dimension reduction. Experimental results proved that the Gabor-SIFT method has higher matching accuracy and less matching time than typical SIFT method, and is suitable for tire indentation mark matching.

2. High-level semantic learning

Machine learning techniques such as neural network (NN) [26,29], compensatory fuzzy neural network (CFNN) [30], probabilistic latent semantic analysis (PLSA) [34], sparse representation[34] are used to obtain high-level semantics of tire indentation mark images.

The PLSA method in [34] contains four components including image pre-processing, low-level texture feature extraction, high-level semantic learning and sparse representation based similarity measure. This system is shown to be effective and has been applied into practical applications.

In the pre-processing step, tilt-alignment is first applied on tire indentation marks, then histogram equalization is used to enhance image contrast and minimize the influence of the background on the texture feature of the image. Gaussian filter is then used for image denoising, before local binarization of the image using the Otsu segmentation.

For low-level texture feature extraction, Gabor basis vocabulary is used together with the model of the tire indentation mark. It is observed that Gabor basis is useful in detecting the direction of tire texture and the density of textures. The PLSA is used to derive latent semantics from low-level texture features. More specifically, low-level texture feature of the training images are mapped to the PLSA model to extract the key words of the latent semantic space and those of each of the training image. The collection of the key words forms the key-word dictionary. Next, based on the latent semantic space of the training images, the key word of the query image can be extracted. For image similarity measure, a sparse coding based strategy is designed. First, the query image is represented by the key-word dictionary using sparse coding. It is then compared with the sparse coding of each of the target

2.3 Tire Pattern Retrieval

images, and the coding residual is calculated. The similarity measure between the query image and the target image is obtained by multiplying the coding residual and coding coefficient, which is then used to rank the target images for retrieval output. The PLSA algorithm is tested on 2,976 noisy tire indentation mark images, the retrieval precision is 99.93%. On the actual crime scene investigation data, the experimental results show that the precision is 100% and the recall is 71.4%. It demonstrates the robustness of the proposed algorithm on incomplete and noisy data.

2.3.5 Summary

So far, four categories of tire pattern classification and retrieval have been identified and discussed: tire tread pattern retrieval, tire surface wear feature extraction, video tire pattern retrieval, tire indentation mark retrieval. Table 2-2 summarizes the existing tire pattern retrieval techniques.

Table 2-2 Summary of tire pattern retrieval techniques

Category	Property	Technique	Applications
Tire tread pattern	Original or close to original tire, clear, high resolution	L^a: Texture feature of tire tread pattern: Tamura, SIFT, GLCM, 2D-FFT, DT-CWT, DWT, Curvelet transform, H-SIFT H^b: PCA, SVM, HFPMC, FCM, binary decision tree, Gabor transform	Patent protection, tire brand/source ID, vehicle ID when vehicle itself not recognizable

(Continued)

Category	Property	Technique	Applications
Tire surface wear	Patch of diminished tire pattern, contrast with background tire pattern	L^a: Gray-level thresholding-based Ostu segmentation method, DWT H^b: Adaptive co-training mechanism based on mutual information	Tire brand ID, tire source tracking, assist tire indentation mark analysis
Video tire pattern	Tire silhouette, remote view and low resolution of tire pattern	H^b: PCA, SVM	Additional evidence to tire indentation, rapid classification of video tire pattern
Tire indentation mark	Tire mark on ground, distorted or broken tire pattern	L^a: Edge detection operators (sobel, roberts, log, canny), color space feature (rgb, hsv, ntsc), CV model, SIFT, FFT, Gabor transform H^b: Neural network, compensatory fuzzy neural network, PLSA, sparse representation	Vehicle/driver ID without vehicle

L^a represents low-level texture feature.

H^b represents high-level semantic learning.

2.4 Discussion about Future Research Directions

In terms of low level approaches, spatial methods usually suffer from noise, lighting and distortion while frequency domain approaches are much more robust to these conditions. Although spatial method like SIFT is also robust, however, it's more computationally expensive than frequency methods. For complex data such as forensic data collected on spot of crime scenes, more advanced machine learning techniques such as PCA and SVM can be used.

In most of the research on tire pattern retrieval so far, texture features are the predominant features. However, in many tire patterns, shape features are prominent, therefore, methods like region based segmentation and complex moment features are potential choices for tire pattern analysis.

2.4 Discussion about Future Research Directions

Based on the survey as well as the demand from real-world applications, this section discusses the research tendency in tire pattern retrieval, and suggests two promising research directions.

2.4.1 Standard test dataset and performance evaluation

There is so far no standard test set in tire pattern retrieval, and researchers usually build their own small datasets, and the results may not be convincing when the algorithm is applied on large scale database. Deep learning [64,65] which has been proved to be effective for image classification tasks, requires large training set. Hence, there is high need to set up standard test set for researchers in this field. Performance evaluation standard is also needed for convenience in performance comparison.

2.4.2 Matching between tire indentation mark and tire tread pattern

In practical application scenario, it happens that only tire indentation mark image is available without any information on tire tread (for example when surveillance videos are not available). How to identify tire tread pattern using indentation mark image is a topic of practical value. It deserves to study the matching relationship between tire indentation marks and tire tread pattern models[11,37]. What makes this task difficult is that tire indentation information varies with the indentation carries such as land, snow, etc. Deep learning could be an effective tool in learning this relationship. However, again, large scale training set is needed at first place.

2.5 Conclusions

Tire pattern retrieval is an important research area in both commercial and forensic applications. In this chapter, we have conducted a comprehensive survey on the state of the art techniques on tire pattern classification and retrieval. It is found that there are generally four categories of tire pattern image retrieval: tire tread pattern retrieval, tire surface wear feature extraction, video tire pattern retrieval and tire indentation mark retrieval. Different approaches and techniques in each of the four categories have been discussed in details, their pros and cons have been identified.

It has been found that a standard database is yet to be created to include large variety of tire patterns for the research experiment and evaluation. There also needs a systematic evaluation on existing techniques and approaches on tire pattern image retrieval. Although texture features have been predominantly used in existing approaches, other techniques such as color and shape features should also be investigated.

References

[1] LIU Y, FAN J L, LI Z, et al. Case study on content-based image retrieval for crime scene investigation image database[J]. Journal of Xi'an University of Posts and Telecommunications, 2015, 20 (3): 11-20.

[2] QIAN B Z. China's first tire pattern patent database operation [J]. Rubber science and technology, 2015, 13(1): 47.

[3] LIU Y, YAN H Y. A rotation-invariant texture feature extraction method for tire pattern image[J]. Journal of Xi'an University of Posts and Telecommunications, 2015, 20 (6): 10-13.

[4] LIU Y, ZHANG D, LU G, et al. A survey of content-based image retrieval with high-level semantics[J]. Pattern recognition, 2007, 40(1): 262-282.

[5] MICHALIKOVA A, VAGAC M. A tire tread pattern detection based on fuzzy logic[C]. Proceedings of the 11th International Conference Flexible Query Answering Systems, Cracow, Poland, 2016: 381-388.

[6] COLBRY D, CHERBA D, LUCHINI J. Pattern recognition for classification and matching of car tires[J]. Tire science & technology, 2005, 33(1): 2-17.

[7] WEI D, PHLYPO R, ADALI T. Adaptive feature split selection for co-training: Application to tire irregular wear classification[C]. IEEE International Conference on Acoustics, Speech and Signal Processing, Vancouver, BC, Canada, 2016: 3497-3501.

[8] JUNG S W, BAE S W, PARK G T. A design scheme for a hierarchical

fuzzy pattern matching classifier and its application to the tire tread pattern recognition[J]. Fuzzy sets & systems, 1994, 65 (2-3): 311-322.

[9] LIU Y, LI Z, GAO Z M. An improved texture feature extraction method for tire tread patterns[J].Intelligence science and big data engineering, Springer Berlin Heidelberg , 2013 , 8261 : 705-713.

[10] LIU Y, LI Z. Study on texture feature extraction from forensic images with watermark[C]. IEEE Conference on Industrial Electronics and Applications (ICIEA), Hangzhou, China, 2014: 1474-1475.

[11] YAN H Y, LIU Y. An improved texture feature extraction method based on radon transform[C].7th IEEE Conference on International Symposium on Computational Intelligence and Design (ISCID), Hangzhou, China, 2015: 481-485.

[12] WANG S, LIU Y, LI D X, et al. An improved SIFT feature extraction method for tire tread patterns retrieval[C].7th IEEE Conference on International Symposium on Computational Intelligence and Design (ISCID), Hangzhou, China, 2014: 539-543.

[13] LI Z, LIU Y, LI D X. A new texture feature extraction method for image retrieval[C]. International Conference on Intelligent Control and Information Processing (ICICIP), Beijing, China, 2013: 482-486.

[14] GUO C, AI M L. Removal of high-density salt and pepper noise of tire trace images based on decision analysis algorithm[J]. Computer engineering & applications, 2012, 48(5): 171-172.

[15] AI M L, GUO C. Tire image enhancement based on frequency division and singular value decomposition[J]. Application research of computers, 2012, 29 (3): 1178-1180.

References

[16] QIAO L, AI M L, GUO C. Application of dual-threshold segmentation based on normalized cut in tire prints and wear characteristics[J]. Computer engineering & applications, 2012, 48(12): 148-152.

[17] AI M L, GUO C. Tire tread pattern recognition based on composite feature extraction and hierarchical support vector machine[J]. Computer engineering & applications, 2013, 49 (20): 179-182.

[18] GUO C. Research on tire prints image enhancement and recognition method[D]. Xi'an: Shaanxi Normal University, 2012.

[19] QIAO L. Research on tire prints image enhancement method[D]. Xi'an: Shaanxi Normal University, 2011.

[20] QIAO L, LIU J H, XUE Y F. X-ray tire image enhancement processing research[J]. Journal of Changzhi University, 2012, 29 (5): 7-29.

[21] WANG Z. Trace ability technologies of suspects' vehicle based on information of tire[D]. Changchun: Jilin University, 2012.

[22] WANG Z, LI D. A survey of vehicle tire prints inspection and identification technology[J]. Highways, automotive application, 2009, 2(2): 50-53.

[23] CHEN Q, LI J, WANG S W, et al. Automatic vehicle classification by radiated noise of vehicles based on AR model[J].Journal of Wuhan University of Technology, 2008, 37(2): 325-328.

[24] ZHANG H X. Study on tire marks image processing and recognition algorithm[D]. Changchun: Jilin University, 2011.

[25] TANG Y S, LI J, YAN S S. Estimating for escaping accident vehicle types using tire trace width[J]. Journal of liaoning institute of technology, 2005, 25 (5): 338-340.

[26] CHEN Q, LI J, WU X, et al. Tire imprint discernment algorithm and ex-

ample analysis[J]. Journal of Jilin University of Technology, 2015, 35 (1): 39-43.

[27] ZHANG H X. Tire trace image sharpening[J]. Police technology, 2015, 5(5): 81-83.

[28] WANG Z, WANG Y P, LI S W. Image matching algorithm for tire impression based on SIFT-Gabor transform[J]. Guangxue Jingmi Gongcheng/ Optics and precision engineering, 2011, 19 (2): 291-297.

[29] CHEN Q, LI J, WU X. Tire prints image recognition based on wavelet transform [C]. International Conference on International Highway Safety Symposium (IHSS), 2004.

[30] YAN S S. Study on intelligent identification system of tire marks at the road traffic accident scene[D]. Changchun: Jilin University, 2003.

[31] WANG Z, LI S, WANG Y. Tire-imprints image enhancement algorithm based on wavelet transformation[C]. IEEE International Conference on Optoelectronics and Image Processing (ICOIP), Haikou, China, 2010: 666-670.

[32] LIN L, SUN J, WANG Z, et al. Recognition method and application to classify a tire image combined curve evolution and characteristic matching[J]. Chinese journal of scientific instrument, 2011, 32(S1): 129-132.

[33] WANG Z, WANG Y, LI S. Tire impressions image segmentation algorithm based on C-V model without re-initialization[C]. IEEE 3rd International Conference on Communication Software and Networks (ICCSN), Xi'an, China, 2011: 541-545.

[34] YU Q. Research on scene tire tread pattern retrieval algorithm[D]. Dalian: Dalian Maritime University, 2015.

References

[35] ZHANG C, CHENG Y H, YIN H.Modified threshold algorithm for feature extraction of tire surface wear[J]. Journal of Beijing Jiaotong University, 2007, 31(2): 57-61.

[36] ZHANG C, CHENG Y H. A hybrid template match approach based on wavelet analysis and threshold segmentation for detecting tire surface wear[C]. IEEE International Conference on Control and Automation (ICCA), Guangzhou, China, 2007: 1079 1084.

[37] ZHANG C. Research on graphical analysis method for tire wear[D]. Beijing: Beijing Jiaotong University, 2008.

[38] BULAN O, BEMAL E A, LOCE R P, et al. Tire classification from still images and video[C].15th International IEEE Conference on Intelligent Transportation Systems, Proceedings, Anchorage, AK, USA, 2012: 485-490.

[39] Center for Image and Information Processing of Xi'an University of Posts and Telecommunication (CIIP), CIIP tire pattern database, Tire Pattern Image Data. [2018-06-25]. http://www.user.qzone.qq.com/3225702926/2.

[40] TIRE RACK in USA, Tire Image Database, Tire Pattern Data. [2018-06-26]. http//www.Tirerack.com.

[41] WEI N, GENG G H, ZHOU Q M. An overview of performance evaluation in content-based image retrieval[J]. Journal of image & graphics, 2004, 9(11): 1271-1276.

[42] DING N N. Research on image registration based on feature points[D]. Changchun: Changchun Institute of Optics, Fine Mechanics and Physics, Chinese Academy of Science, 2012.

[43] WANG H, WANG X Q. Fingerprint identification index and testing method[J]. Computer era, 2007, 3(1): 49-50.

[44] Qi Y L. A Relevance Feedback Retrieval Method Based on Tamura Texture[C]. Second International Symposium on Knowledge Acquisition and modeling, Wuhan, China, 2009: 174-177.

[45] JIA S Y, MA J T. Tire pattern retrieval based on wavelet transform and gray level co-occurrence matrix[J]. Computer measurement & control, 2016, (16): 210-213.

[46] HAO Y B, WANG R L, JUN M A, et al. Image retrieval based on improved Tamura texture features[J]. Science of surveying & mapping, 2010, 35(4) : 136-138.

[47] SANDIRASEGARAM N, ENGLISH R. Comparative analysis of feature extraction (2D FFT and wavelet) and classification (Lp metric distances, MLP NN, and HNeT) algorithms for SAR imagery[J]. Defense and security, proceedings of SPIE-the international society for optical engineering, 2005, 5808 (6B): L724-L727.

[48] HELGASON S.The Radon Transform[M]. Boston: Birkhäuser, 1980.

[49] CANDES E J. Ridgelets: theory and applications[D]. California: Stanford University, 1998.

[50] KINGSBUR N. Complex wavelets for shift invariant analysis and filtering of signals[J]. Applied & computational harmonic analysis, 2001, 10 (3): 234-253.

[51] MORTAZAYI S H, SHAHARTASH M S. Comparing denoising performance of DWT, WPT, SWT and DT-CWT for Partial Discharge signals[C]. 2008 43rd International Universities Power Engineering

Conference (UPEC), Technological Educational Institute, Padova, Italy, 2008: 1-6.

[52] CADES E J, DONOHO D L. Continuous curvelet transform: II. Discretization and frames[J]. Applied and computational harmonic analysis, 2005, 19(2): 198-222.

[53] CANDES E J, DONOHO D L. Curvelets and reconstruction of images from noisy radon data[J]. The international society for optical engineering, 2000, 4119: 108-117.

[54] MINHAS R, MOHAMMED A A, WU Q M J. Shape from focus using fast discrete curvelet transform[J]. Pattern recognition, 2011, 44(4): 839-853.

[55] HEIL C, WALNUT D F. Continuous and discrete wavelet transfor[J]. Society for industrial and applied mathematics, 1989, 31 (4): 628-666.

[56] LIU Y, YAN H Y, LIM K P. Study on rotation-invariant texture feature extraction for tire pattern retrieval[J]. Multidimensional systems & signal processing, 2017, 28 (2): 757-770.

[57] SELESNICK I W, BARANIUK R G, KINGBURY N C. The dual-tree complex wavelet transform[J]. IEEE signal processing magazine, 2005, 22(6): 123-151.

[58] HUANG D Y, HU W C, WANG Y W, et al. Recognition of tire tread patterns based on gabor wavelets and support vector machine[C]. 2010 2nd International Conference on Computational Collective Intelligence-Technologies and Applications (ICCCI), Kaohsiung, 2010: 92-101.

[59] ZHANG C, CHENG Y H. A quadric image segmentation for the feature extraction of tire surface wear[C].2006 6th International Conference on Intelligent Systems Design and Applications (ISDA), Jinan, China, 2006:

457-462.

[60] MARIMONT D H, WANDELL B A. Matching color images: The effects of axial chromatic aberration[J].Journal of the optical society of America A, 1994, 11(12): 3113-3122.

[61] THIBOS L N, BRADLEY A, STILL D L, et al. Theory and measurement of ocular chromatic aberration[J]. Vision research, 1990, 30(1): 33-49.

[62] NIU J L. Study on tire imprint recognition based on FFT image difference[J]. Computer digit engine, 2011, 39 (5): 139-141.

[63] WANG S D, XIAO J Y, LIU Z Q, et al. Study on tire imprint image recognition based on FFT image differencing algorithm[C]. 5th International Conference on Fuzzy Systems and Knowledge Discovery (FSKD), Shandong, China, 2008: 504-508.

[64] HINTON G E, OSINDERO S, TEH Y W. A fast learning algorithm for deep belief nets[J]. Neural computation, 2006, 18(7): 1527-1554.

[65] WSHAH S, XU B, BULAN O, et al. Deep learning architectures for domain adaptation in HOV/HOT lane enforcement[C]. IEEE Winter Conference on Applications of Computer Vision (WACV), Lake Placid, NY, USA, 2016: 1-7.

Chapter 3

A Modified Tamura Feature for Tire Pattern Image Description

3.1 Introduction of Tamura Feature

Texture is an important feature of image which describes the spatial distribution of different elements (pixels). Texture feature describes the homogeneity of image surface not depending on the color and brightness information. As texture feature can reflect the global property and local structure of an image, it has been widely used in image analysis for applications such as image database retrieval and image recognition[1,2].

Many texture feature extraction methods have been designed for CBIR, including Wavelet-based texture feature, Tamura texture, feature gray-level co-occurrence matrix and so on. Different from other texture features, Tamura texture features are calculated based on human visual perception system and are commonly used for image retrieval. In [3], the author presented a modified Tamura texture feature. This chapter presents a method which further improves the method in [3] .

Contrast, as a type of Tamura texture feature, is a global variable which can well describe the statistical distribution of the brightness in the entire image, but can not reflect the local brightness information of the image. This chapter proposes an improved method, which makes use of the statistical moments of intensity histogram to extract more information from the image. Tested on a tire tread pattern dataset, the proposed method provides better retrieval performance compared with existing methods. Hence, it is concluded that the proposed method is effective in texture feature description especially for type texture, due to the fact that more intensity information is exploited.

The rest of this chapter is organized as follows. In Section 3.2, we review Tamura texture feature and describe the method proposed. Section 3.3 presents the experimental results on tire pattern data set. Section 3.4 concludes this chapter.

3.2 Modification of Tamura Texture Feature

3.2.1 Tamura texture feature

In 1978, Tamura proposed six texture features according to human visual perception, namely, coarseness, contrast, directionality, line likeness, regularity, roughness. Experimentally, the first three components correlate better with human perception than the last three. In addition, the last three features are highly correlated with the first three features and are not much to the effective for description the texture feature. For these reasons, the first three Tamura feature are widely used for image retrieval[4,5].

1. Coarseness

Coarseness as the basic feature of the Tamura texture, reflects the largest size of the texture elements, even where a smaller texture exists. The larger the coarseness value is, the rougher the texture is. For the

3.2 Modification of Tamura Texture Feature

different texture pattern structures, the more primitive size or the less primitive number of repetitions, gives people the impression of roughness. The essence of calculating the value of coarseness is the sliding value of the pixels with different size windows. It can be summarized as follows.

Step 1: Taking the average at every pixel over neighborhoods whose sizes are the power of 2. The average over the neighborhood of size $2^k \times 2^k (k = 0, 1, 2, 3, 4, 5)$ at every pixel is:

$$A_k(x, y) = \sum_{i=x-2^{k-1}}^{i=x+2^{k-1}-1} \sum_{j=y-2^{k-1}}^{j=y+2^{k-1}-1} g(i,j)/2^{2k} \qquad (3\text{-}1)$$

where $g(i, j)$ is the gray-level at (x, y).

Step 2: For each pixel, calculating the differences between the not overlapping neighborhoods on horizontal and vertical directions:

$$E_{k,h}(x, y) = |A_k(x + 2^{k-1}, y) - A_k(x + 2^{k-1}, y)|$$
$$E_{k,v}(x, y) = |A_k(x, y + 2^{k+1}) - A_k(x, y - 2^{k-1})| \qquad (3\text{-}2)$$

Step 3: For each pixel, selecting the best size which gives the highest output value:

$$S_{\text{best}}(x, y) = 2^k + 1 \qquad (3\text{-}3)$$

where k maximizes E in either direction:

$$E_k(x, y) = \max(E_{k,h}(x, y), E_{k,v}(x, y))_E$$

Step 4: Taking the average of S_{best} over the picture to be the coarseness measure F_{crs}:

$$F_{\text{crs}} = \sum_{i=1}^{m} \sum_{j=1}^{n} S_{\text{best}}(i, j)/(m \cdot n) \qquad (3\text{-}4)$$

where m and n are the effective size of the image. Apparently, F_{crs} describes the rough grain size characteristic of the texture image, but when textons of different sizes exist in the image, coarseness as defined in formula (3-4) can't well reflect the texture characteristic of the image as there is information loss. An improved method was proposed in [1] which describes the distribution of S_{best} using the histogram of coarseness, not just taking the average of coarseness. The histogram of coarseness conveys the information of textons of different sizes in the image and thus reflects the texture features of different regions. Thus, it brings performance improvement in the image retrieval.

2. Directionality

Direction is the most basic feature of the image which contains a large amount of image information. It describes globally how the texture in the image is distributed or concentrated along certain orientations. The calculation of directionality can be summarized as following.

Step 1: Calculating the gradient vector at each pixel which includes its modulus $|\Delta G|$ and the edge directionality θ as,

$$|\Delta G| = (|\Delta H| + |\Delta V|)/2 \tag{3-5}$$

$$\theta = \tan^{-1}(\Delta V/\Delta H) + \pi/2 \tag{3-6}$$

where ΔH and ΔV are the horizontal and vertical elements, calculated as the convolution of the image with the following 3×3 operators:

$$\begin{vmatrix} -1 & 0 & 1 \\ -1 & 0 & 1 \\ -1 & 0 & 1 \end{vmatrix} \quad \begin{vmatrix} 1 & 1 & 1 \\ 0 & 0 & 0 \\ -1 & -1 & -1 \end{vmatrix} \tag{3-7}$$

Step 2: Counting all pixels with $|\Delta G| \geq t$ and quantizing θ by $(2k-1)\pi/2n \leq \theta < (2k+1)\pi/2n$, we obtain the number of the points $N_\theta(k)$ which satisfy the above constraints. Then, building the edge probabilities histogram HD.

3.2 Modification of Tamura Texture Feature

$$\text{HD}(k) = N_\theta(k) / \sum_{i=0}^{n-1} N_\theta(i), k = 0, 1, \cdots, n-1 \qquad (3\text{-}8)$$

In our experiments, we used $n = 36$ and $t = 12$.

Step 3: This measure can be defined as follows:

$$F_{\text{dir}} = \sum_{p}^{n_p} \sum_{\phi \in w_p} (\phi - \phi_p)^2 H_D(\phi) \qquad (3\text{-}9)$$

where p is the peak value of histogram, n_p are all the peak values of the histogram. For each p, w_p represents all the bins which include it, and ϕ_p is the bin which has the highest peak value.

Directionality as a global property over the given region, measures the total degree of directionality, but can not effectively reflect the local different orientations or patterns. As in [3], the author uses Fourier Transform to convert HD to frequency domain. Then choose the modulus instead of F_{dir} to describe the texture. We can see the result is very promising. The advantage of thus method is that it can eliminate the phase difference between the image histograms and thus the texture feature is rotation-invariant.

3. Contrast

Contrast reflects the statistical distribution of brightness of pixels in the image and is determined by four factors: gray-level dynamic range, polarization degree of the white and black part in the histogram, sharpness of the edge, repeat model cycles. Often we define contrast as following,

$$F_{\text{con}} = \delta / (a_4)^n \qquad (3\text{-}10)$$

where $a_4 = \mu_4/\delta_4$, μ_4 is the fourth moments, δ^2 is the variance. Experimentally, $n = 1/4$ was the best value obtained by Tamura et al.

3.2.2 Modification

From formula (3-10) we can see contrast is a global variable which can well describe the statistical distribution of the brightness in the entire image, but can not reflect the local brightness information of the image. We propose an improved method, which makes use of the statistical moments of intensity histogram to extract more information from the image. Because of the images which we used for experiments are segments from the whole image of the tire type patterns, so we take these images as a big block. We use the following features to describe the intensity distribution in the image:

Mean: a measure of average intensity, which represents the brightness information of image.

$$m = \sum_{i=0}^{L-1} z_i p(z_i) \tag{3-11}$$

where z_i is a random variable intensity, $p(z_i)$ is the histogram of the intensity levels, L is the number of possible intensity levels.

Standard deviation: measure the contrast of gray level intensities as:

$$\delta = \sqrt{\mu_2(z)} = \sqrt{\delta^2} \tag{3-12}$$

where δ^2 is the variance, and is the second moments $\mu_2(z)$.

Smoothness: using the standard deviation value, measure the relative smoothness of the intensity.

$$R = 1 - 1/(1 + \delta^2) \tag{3-13}$$

Third moment: measures the skewness of a histogram.

$$\mu_3 = \sum_{i=0}^{L-1} (z_i - m)^3 p(z_i) \tag{3-14}$$

3.2 Modification of Tamura Texture Feature

Uniformity: measures the distribution of intensity level:

$$U = \sum_{i=0}^{L-1} p^2(z_i) \qquad (3\text{-}15)$$

Entropy: measures the randomness pixels value of the distribution

$$e = -\sum_{i=0}^{L-1} p(z_i)\text{lb } p(z_i) \qquad (3\text{-}16)$$

The three images in Fig.3 1(from left to right) are examples of images of smooth, coarse and periodic tire tread patterns. The histogram of these images are shown in Fig. 3-2. We can use equation (3-11) to equation (3-16) to obtain six different values to construct a new texture feature: $T = [m, \delta, R, \mu_3, U, e]$. The corresponding texture feature values for the three images in Fig.3-1 are given in Table 3-1.

(a) type1   (b) type2   (c) type3

Fig. 3-1 Examples of different types of tire patterns

Apparently, the results are in general agreement with the texture content of the respective images. For example, because the values of the pixels in coarser region are more random than the values in other regions, so the mean, entropy, contrast of the coarser region is higher than those of other regions. But, this region is the least smooth and the least uniform. As the histogram of the coarse image evident shows: the greatest lack of symmetry with respect to the location of the mean value, and others image are better[6].

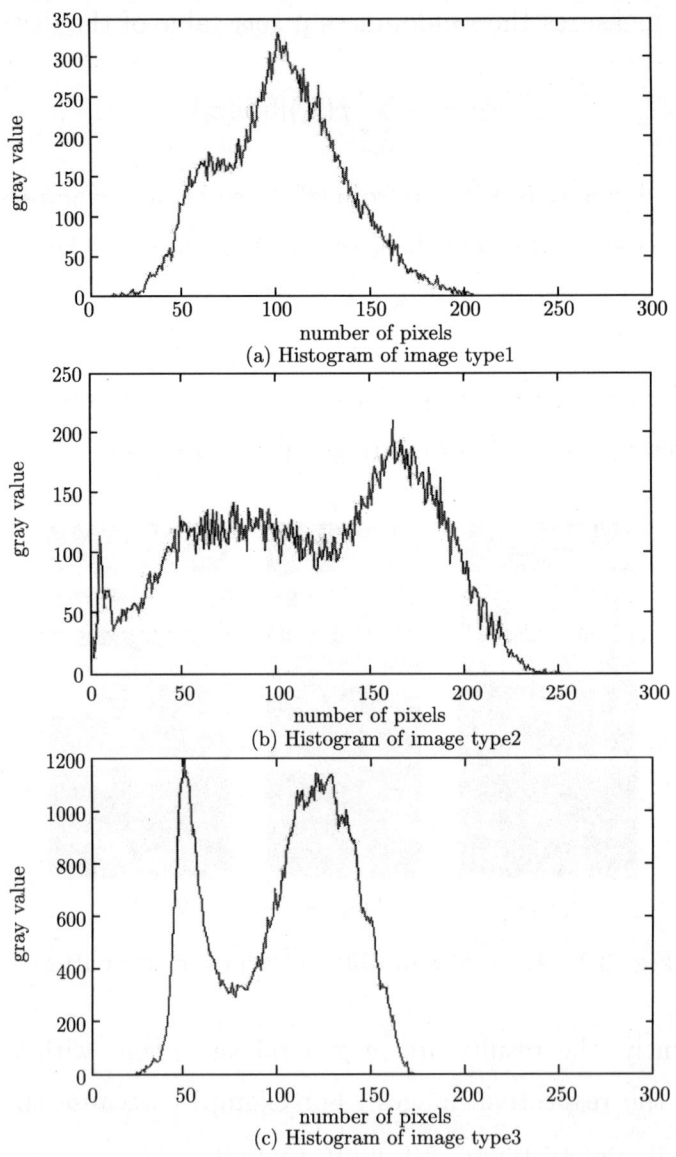

Fig. 3-2 Histogram corresponding to the images in Fig.3-1

Table 3-1 Texture features for the images shown in Fig.3-1

Texture	Smooth	Coarse	Periodic
Mean	101.5387	117.4975	101.3637
Standard deviation	32.5610	56.9236	34.4564
Smoothness	0.0160	0.0475	0.0179
Third moment	0.0738	−0.5251	−0.2076
Uniformity	0.0087	0.0051	6.0095
Entropy	7.0423	7.7167	6.8748

3.3 Experimental Results

In order to verify the performance of the proposed algorithm in image retrieval, we use a tire tread pattern dataset from a public security criminal investigation database. We selected 40 categories and each has 5 relevant images. We use inner query to test retrieval performance, that is, we select an image from the database as query. Texture features of all the images in the dataset are extracted and normalized. Image similarity measure is defined as the Euclidean distance between texture feature vectors as below.

$$d_{\mathrm{c}} = \sqrt{\sum_{i=1}^{L} [t_{\mathrm{q}}(i) - t_{\mathrm{d}}^{j}(i)]^2} \quad (3\text{-}17)$$

where d_{c} is the similarity between feature vectors, $t_{\mathrm{q}}(i)$ is the feature vector of the query image. $t_{\mathrm{d}}^{j}(i)$ is feature vector of the database image, L is the length of feature vector.

In order to further improve the accuracy of retrieval, we integrate coarseness, directionality and contrast together as texture feature of images as:

$$S = (1/3) \times d_{\text{coa}} + (1/3) \times d_{\text{dir}} + (1/3) \times d_{\text{con}} \quad (3\text{-}18)$$

We use precision to evaluate the performance of different texture features for image retrieval, which is defined as:

$$\text{precision} = s/k \quad (3\text{-}19)$$

Where s is the number of relevant images retrieved, k is the total number of images returned[1].

Compared with other similarity measure methods such as Canberra distance which are often used, in our experiments, Euclidean distance has been proved to be more effective in image similarity measure for retrieval purpose, with higher retrieval accuracy and better ranking order. In addition, Euclidean distance measure is simple to implement.

Retrieval performance of three texture features are compared in our experiments: the proposed method as described above, the method provide in [3], and wavelet-based texture features. Wavelet transform is often used for texture feature extraction. In our experiments, we applied 2-level wavelet transform with Bior2.2 basis to obtain texture feature of 7 dimensions. Details of wavelet-based texture feature can be found in [2]. Given a set of queries, retrieval performance of three texture features are compared. Experimentally, the proposed algorithm provides retrieval results better than other two methods, as shown in Fig.3-3.

From Fig.3-3, we can conclude that the proposed method provides the best retrieval performance. For example, when $k=10$, using our method, there is a significant improvement in retrieval precision from 41.50% to 45.75%. And we can see from the trend of the curves that the rank of the returned images has been dramatically improved using our method.

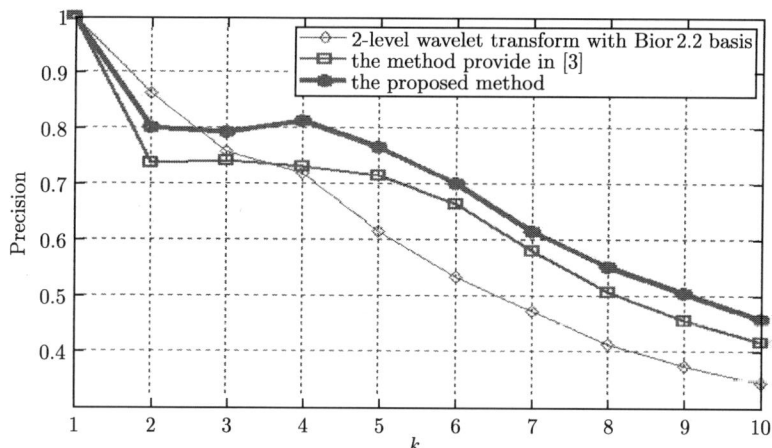

Fig. 3-3 Retrieval performance comparison

3.4 Conclusions

In this chapter, a new texture feature extraction method based on Tamura texture feature has been proposed for tire tread pattern image retrieval. The proposed method made use of the statistical moments of intensity histogram experimental results proved that this method is not only efficient in computation, but also provides promising retrieval performance.

References

[1] LIU Y, ZHANG D, LU G J, et al. A survey of content-based image retrieval with high level semantics[J]. Pattern recognition, 2007, 40(1): 262-282.

[2] LIU J M. Technology of texture feature extraction based on wavelet[J]. Computer engineering and design, 2007, 28(13): 3141-3144.

[3] HAO Y B, WANG R L, MA J, et al. Image retrieval based on improved Tamura texture features[J]. Science of surveying and mapping, 2010, 35(4): 136-138.

[4] QI Y L. A Relevance Feedback Retrieval Method Based on Tamura Texture[C]. Second International Symposium on Knowledge Acquisition and modeling, Wuhan, China, 2009: 174-177.

[5] TAMURA H, MORI S, YAMWAKI T. Texture features corresponding to visual perception[J]. IEEE transactions on systems, man and cybernetics, 1978, 8(6): 460-473.

[6] RAFAEL C, GONZALEZ, RCHARD E, et al. Digital Image Processing Using MATLAB[M]. Beijing: Publishing House of Electronics Industry, 2009.

Chapter 4

H-SIFT: SIFT from High-Frequency Information of Tire Pattern Images

4.1 Introduction of SIFT Feature

Compared to geometric shape, texture information and color histogram, scale invariant points have stronger ability to adapt a variety of image transformation as a kind of local features. So in recent years, the scale invariant feature points extraction algorithm and its application have become a research hotspot in the field of image processing[1-8].

At present, the scale invariant feature points extraction algorithms researched widely include Harris-Laplacian algorithm and SIFT algorithm[2], etc. Harris-Laplacian algorithm is a kind of feature points extraction algorithm based on Harris angular points. This descriptor has a simple computation and a low dimension, but it is more sensitive to noises. So it needs much more experimental data to estimate the covariance matrix. SIFT algorithm is a approximate calculation of the normalized Laplacian operator in the scale space. The descriptor used in SIFT algorithm has a 128-dimensional feature vector space by calculating gradient direction histogram of the feature points in the local field, and good results have been achieved. SIFT feature keeps invariance to rotation, zooming in and out, brightness variation, and it also has a degree of stability to perspective changes, affine transform and noises[2,5]. Mikolajczyk and others made a comparison for a variety of descriptors, and the results show that the descriptor based on SIFT has the best performance[3]. However, these descriptors are 128-D. Although the precision of image retrieval based on SIFT feature is very high, it takes a long time and the efficiency is low. In order to solve the problem, this chapter proposes an algorithm based on 2-level wavelet transform. In this algorithm, taking 2-level wavelet transform to the image , then setting its low-frequency sub-band to zero and reconstructing the image by its 6 high-frequency sub-bands, finally, retrieving the reconstructed image by SIFT feature. This method can reduce SIFT feature points extracted in an image and keep the detail information in the image from losing, so it has little influence on the precision. Tested on a tire tread pattern dataset in public security forensic image data, the proposed algorithm in this chapter is found to be able to improve the image retrieval efficiency obviously. The rest of this chapter is organized as follows. Section 4.2 reviews SIFT feature and Section 4.3 describes the method we proposed named H-SIFT. Section 4.4 presents the experimental results on tire pattern image dataset. Section 4.5 concludes this chapter and suggest future research directions

4.2 Review of SIFT Feature

In 1999 at British Columbia University, Professor Lowe summarized existing feature detection methods based on invariant technology, and put forward a kind of local characteristics of the image based on scale

4.2 Review of SIFT Feature

space(SIFT), which can keep invariant to image zooming in and out, rotation and even affine transformation[2]. The algorithm was improved in 2004. The essence of the SIFT algorithm can be classified as a problem to find the feature points in different scale space[2]. The implementation steps of SIFT algorithm can be summarized as in Fig.4-1[2,6,7].

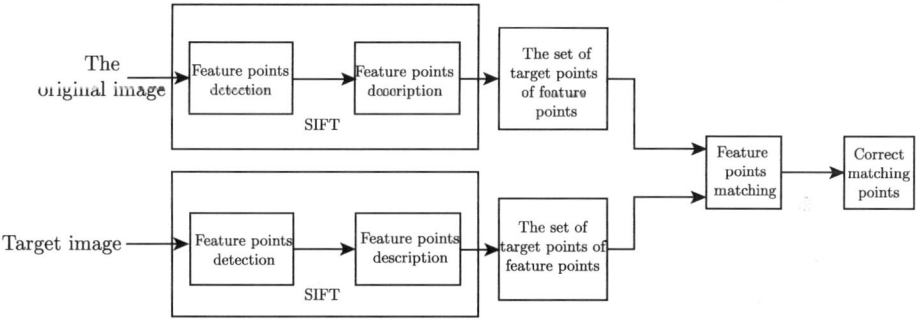

Fig. 4-1 The brief state of implementation steps of SIFT algorithm

To realize the object recognition by SIFT algorithm mainly has three working procedures: ① extracting key points; ② adding detailed information (local features) to the key points; ③ finding out couples of feature points matching each other by comparing the feature points of both images (the key points with feature vectors), in the meantime, the corresponding relationship between the images has been established[2].

4.2.1 Scale space and relevant concepts

Scale space theory is first presented in 1962, its main idea is to obtain the scale space sequences of one image in multi-scale by taking scale transformation to the original image, and extract the main outline of these sequences in scale space, which is used as a kind of feature vectors to realize edge and corner points detection and feature detection in different resolutions[9]. The scale space of an image is composed of various representations of the image under different resolutions. The representation of an image under one resolution can be obtained through the convolution of the Gaussian kernel. And the scale size of the image is represented by the standard deviation σ of the Gaussian kernel. Studies show that the Gaussian kernel is the only kernel to produce multi-scale spaces. Therefore, the scale space of an image is a 3-dimensional space which consists of X, Y and σ. Among them, the X, Y decides location and σ decides resolution. The closer to the bottom the image scale level σ is, the clearer the image is, the closer to the top the image scale level σ is, the fuzzier the image is [2, 9].

The scale space $L(X, Y, \sigma)$ of an image is defined as a convolution operation of the original image $I(X, Y)$ and a scale variable 2-dimension gaussian function $G(X, Y, \sigma)$ as follows [2], [6] and [7].

Gaussian function:

$$G(x, y, \sigma) = \frac{1}{2\pi\sigma^2} \exp\left(-\frac{(x-x_i)^2 + (y-y_i)^2}{2\sigma^2}\right) \qquad (4\text{-}1)$$

Scale space:

$$L(x, y, \sigma) = G(x, y, \sigma) \cdot I(x, y) \qquad (4\text{-}2)$$

The Gaussian blur as in Fig.4-2 is often used in reducing the size of an image. The image is usually processed by low-pass filters before making the under sampling. And it can insure that the false high-frequency information will not happen in the sampling image. The gaussian low-pass filter function is as follows:

$$G(r) = \frac{1}{2\pi\sigma^2} \exp\left(-\frac{r^2}{2\sigma^2}\right) \qquad (4\text{-}3)$$

r is the fuzzy radius,

$$r = \sqrt{x^2 + y^2} \qquad (4\text{-}4)$$

4.2 Review of SIFT Feature

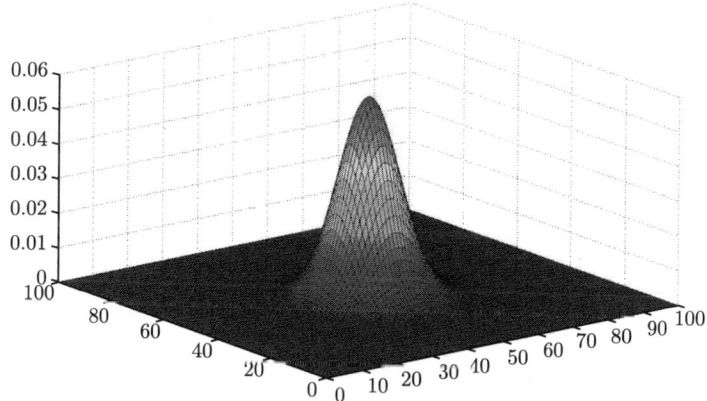

Fig. 4-2 Gaussian blur

4.2.2 The model of Gaussian pyramid and difference of Gaussian pyramid

The build process of Gaussian pyramid can be divided into two steps:

(1) Doing Gaussian smoothing to the image;

(2) Doing decimation to the image.

In order to let the scale reflect the continuity, the Gaussian filter is added to the simple sampling. An image can produce several groups of images, and a group of images includes several layers of images. The bottom layer of the last group of images is created by the image whose scale is 2σ in the next group of images, alternately sampled with the factor which is two. And it can keep the continuity of the scale[2,6]. Fig.4-3 shows the model of Gaussian pyramid.

Based on the DOG (difference of Gaussian) operator, we can build difference of Gaussian pyramid[2,6,7]. The pixel value changes of the image can be found by the DOG diagram. If there is no change, there would be no feature point, and the feature points must be the points changed as much as possible. A DOG diagram describes the outline of the target image. Fig.4-4 displays the model of DOG.

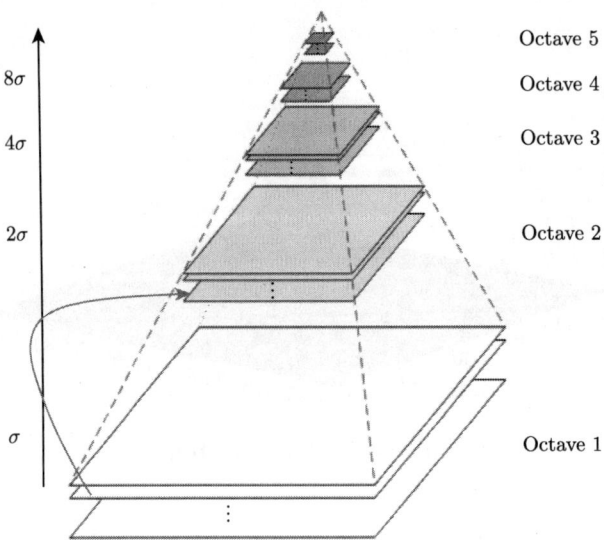

Fig.4-3 The model of Gaussian pyramid

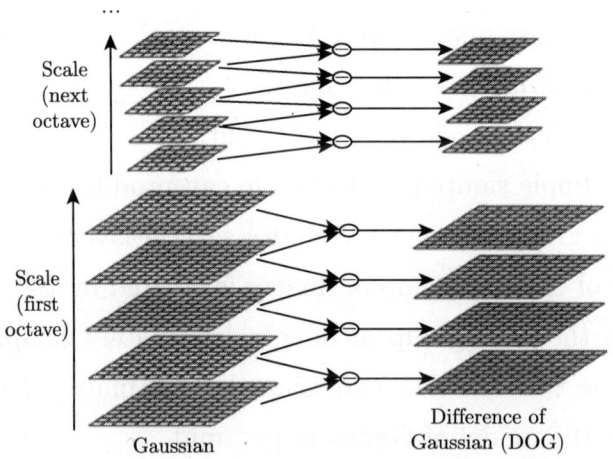

Fig.4-4 The model of DOG

DOG function is as follows.

Scale space:
$$L(x,y,\sigma) = G(x,y,\sigma) \cdot I(x,y) \qquad (4\text{-}5)$$

DOG function:

4.2 Review of SIFT Feature

$$D(x, y, \sigma) = [G(x, y, k\sigma) - G(x, y, \sigma)] \cdot I(x, y)$$
$$= L(x, y, k\sigma) - L(x, y, \sigma) \quad (4\text{-}6)$$

4.2.3 The establishment of the key points

1. The location and scale of the key points

First of all, the feature points have to be located exactly, for which the steps as follows should be done. In order to improve the stability of the key points, the scale space DOG function is needed to be curve fitted[2,8]. Using the Taylor expansion of DOG function in the scale space:

$$D(X) = D + \frac{\partial D^{\mathrm{T}}}{\partial X} X + \frac{1}{2} X^{\mathrm{T}} \frac{\partial^2 D}{\partial X^2} X \frac{-b \pm \sqrt{b^2 - 4ac}}{2a} \quad (4\text{-}7)$$

Its extreme point is

$$\hat{X} = (x, y, \sigma)^{\mathrm{T}} \quad (4\text{-}8)$$

In the process of calculation, the row, column and scale of the image is respectively revised and the revised results are as follows:

$$D(X) = D + \frac{\partial D^{\mathrm{T}}}{\partial X} X + \frac{1}{2} X^{\mathrm{T}} \frac{\partial^2 D}{\partial X^2} X \quad (4\text{-}9)$$

The result is

$$X = -\frac{\partial D^{\mathrm{T}}}{\partial X} \left(\frac{\partial^2 D}{\partial X^2} \right)^{-1} \quad (4\text{-}10)$$

where X is the revised value.

Then put the revised result into the formula (4-9), we can get:

$$D(X) = D + \frac{1}{2} \frac{\partial D^{\mathrm{T}}}{\partial X^{\mathrm{T}}} X \quad (4\text{-}11)$$

The low contrast points should be removed. Lowe's tests[2] showed that all extreme points whose value is less than 0.04 can be abandoned (the range of the pixel gray value is $[0, 1]$).

Except for the low contrast extreme points, the points in the sides of the image also have to be removed because DOG function has a strong edge response on the edge of the image. The peak points of DOG function have larger main curvature in the direction across the edge of the images, and have a smaller principal curvature in the vertical direction. Principal curvature can be obtain by calculating the 2 × 2 Hessian matrix in the position scale of the point, and the derivative can be estimated by the adjacent difference of the sample points.

The Hessian matrix:

$$H = \begin{bmatrix} D_{xx} & D_{xy} \\ D_{xy} & D_{yy} \end{bmatrix} \qquad (4\text{-}12)$$

D_{xx} denotes the image in a certain scale of the DOG pyramid calculating derivative twice in X direction. The principal curvature of D is proportional to the characteristic value of H. So set α to be the largest characteristic value while β to be the smallest one, we can get follows:

Set

$$\alpha = r\beta \qquad (4\text{-}13)$$

$$\frac{\text{Tr}(H)^2}{\text{Det}(H)} = \frac{(\alpha+\beta)^2}{\alpha\beta} = \frac{(r+1)^2}{r} \qquad (4\text{-}14)$$

$$\text{Tr}(H) = D_{xx} + D_{yy} \qquad (4\text{-}15)$$

$$\text{Det}(H) = D_{xx} \times D_{yy} - D_{xy} \times D_{yy} \qquad (4\text{-}16)$$

$(r+1)^2/r$ is the smallest when the two feature values are equal, and it increases with the increase of r. Lowe suggested r take 1 in his paper. And the judgment formula is as follows:

$$\frac{\text{Tr}(H)^2}{\text{Det}(H)} < \frac{(r+1)^2}{r} \qquad (4\text{-}17)$$

When the formula (4-17) occurs, the key point can be reserved, or remove it.

4.2 Review of SIFT Feature

2. The direction of the key points

The direction of the extreme value points is given by calculating the gradient of every extreme value point[2,10]. The gradient of pixel points is represented as follows:

$$\text{grad } I(x,y) = \left(\frac{\partial I}{\partial x}, \frac{\partial I}{\partial y}\right) \tag{4-18}$$

The gradient magnitude:

$$m(x,y) = \sqrt{[L(x+1,y)-L(x-1,y)]^2 + [L(x,y+1)-L(x,y-1)]^2} \tag{4-19}$$

The gradient direction:

$$\theta(x,y) = \tan^{-1}\left[\frac{L(x,y+1)-L(x,y-1)}{L(x+1,y)-L(x-1,y)}\right] \tag{4-20}$$

The gradient of a pixel point constitutes the gradient histogram, which gives the direction of the key points. The key points of an image have been detected up. Every key point has three key information: location, scale and direction, which makes the key point has the translation invariance, scaling invariance and rotation invariance.

4.2.4 The key points matching

Establish key descriptor sets respectively for reference image and observation image, and target recognition is done by comparing the key point descriptors in the two sets[2,7]. The similarity of the descriptors with 128-dimension is measured by the Euclidean distance as follows:

$$d(R_i, S_i) = \sqrt{\sum_{j=1}^{128}(r_{ij}-s_{ij})^2} \tag{4-21}$$

The key descriptor of the reference image:

$$R_i = (r_{i1}, r_{i2}, \cdots, r_{i128}) \tag{4-22}$$

The key descriptor of the observation image:

$$S_i = (s_{i1}, s_{i2}, \cdots, s_{i128}) \qquad (4\text{-}23)$$

If the two key point descriptors can match, $d(R_i, S_j)$ is needed to satisfy:

$$\frac{\text{The nearest point } S_j \text{ to } R_i \text{ in the observation image}}{\text{The second nearest point } S_p \text{ to } R_i \text{ in the observation image}}$$
$$< \text{Threshold} \qquad (4\text{-}24)$$

4.3 Description of the Proposed Method H-SIFT

In order to improve the efficiency of the existing, sparse representation for image is needed to reduce the complexity of the data to improve the calculation speed. And wavelet transform method is a very good image spare representation. The details of the image is concentrated in high frequency whose sub-band coefficient is small after isolated by wavelet transform and the image can be sparse represented. Take 2-level wavelet transform to the image to isolate 6 high frequency sub-bands and 1 low frequency sub-band. In order to take advantage of high frequency information, the low frequency sub-band has to be set zero. And reconstruct the image with the 6 high frequency sub-bands through the reconstruction filter which is corresponded to the decompose filter[5]. This high-frequency reconstructed image is named as H-image. Fig.4-5 explains 2-level wavelet decomposition and synthesis procedure.

The wavelet function is

$$\varphi(x) = \sqrt{2} \sum_k h(k)\varphi(2x - k)$$
$$\psi(x) = \sqrt{2} \sum_k g(k)\varphi(2x - k) \qquad (4\text{-}25)$$

4.3 Description of the Proposed Method H-SIFT

The scale function is

$$g(k) = (-1)^k h(1-k) \tag{4-26}$$

SIFT feature can be obtained from the H-image as the H-SIFT feature of the tire pattern. Fig.4-6(a) shows an original tire tread

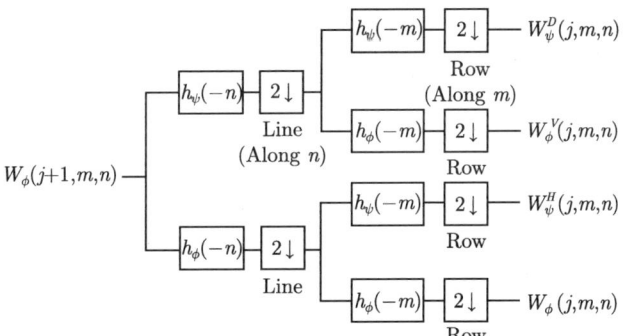

(a) 2-level wavelet decomposition process map

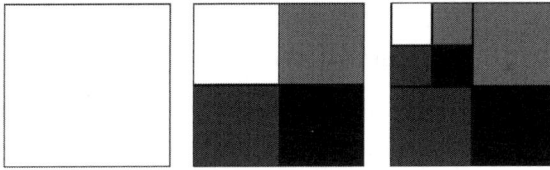

(b) 2-level wavelet decomposition sketch map

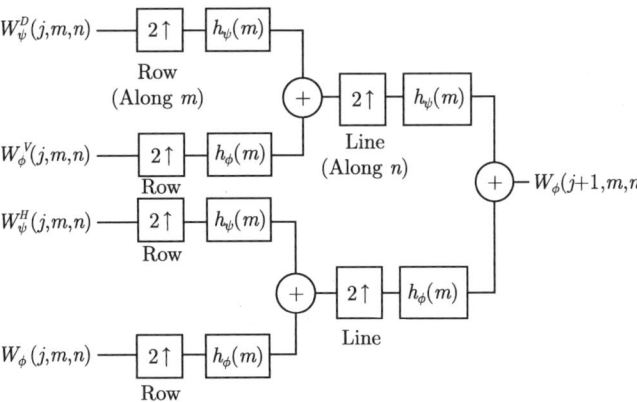

(c) 2-level wavelet synthesis process map

Fig. 4-5 2-level wavelet decomposition and synthesis map

pattern, the corresponding 2-level DWT decomposition result is displayed in Fig4-6(b), Fig4-6(c) is the resulted H-image.

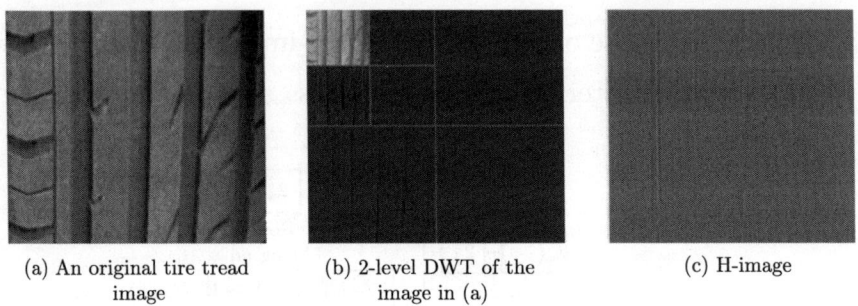

(a) An original tire tread image (b) 2-level DWT of the image in (a) (c) H-image

Fig. 4-6   An example of H-image

4.4   Experimental Results

To verify the performance of the proposed algorithm in image retrieval, a set of experiments are carried out on a tire pattern image dataset which contains 200 images in 40 categories with 5 similar images in each category. In our experiments, according to the proposed H-SIFT algorithm in this chapter, 2-level wavelet decomposition and reconstruction is used to reconstruct high frequency images (H-image) from the 200 original tire tread patterns images. Then H-SIFT feature is calculated from each of the 200 H-images and used for image similarity measure defined by Euclidean distance between image feature vectors.

Average prevision and average retrieval time are calculated to compare the performance of the proposed H-SIFT feature with the original SIFT feature. The results are shown in Fig. 4-7 and Table 4-1, respectively.

Fig.4-7 compares the precision of the four methods (H-SIFT, SIFT, discrete wavelet-transform (DWT) based texture feature and Tamura

4.4 Experimental Results

feature[11,12]), and Table 4-1 compares the average time spent for 200 queries. It can be concluded that the original SIFT provides the best retrieval performance but it spends much more time than other methods. The proposed H-SIFT method greatly reduces the computational load of SIFT with some loss in retrieval precision. However, H-SIFT still has obviously better retrieval performance than DWT feature and Tamura feature, with less computation cost. Hence, the effectiveness of the proposed H-SIFT method is proved.

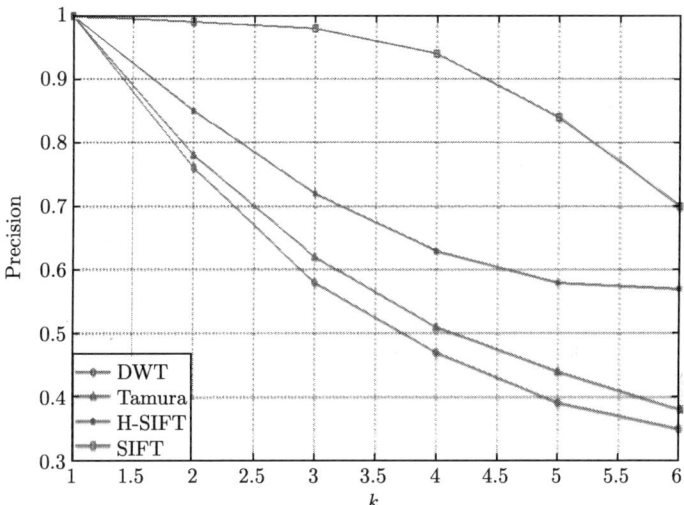

Fig. 4-7 Retrieval performance comparison

Table 4-1 Average time spent by different methods

Feature	Average retrieval time
SIFT	21.501987s
H-SIFT	0.421987s
DWT	2.087622s
Tamura	4.766650s

4.5 Conclusions

This chapter presented an improved SIFT feature extraction method for tire patterns based on wavelet transform. This method made use of image high frequency reconstruction based on 2-level wavelet decomposition and reconstruction, in order to reduce of size of SIFT feature to improve retrieval speed. Experimental results proved that the proposed method not only provides good retrieval performance, but also significantly improves retrieval speed. In our future work, it deserves further effort to optimize the proposed method for application in larger dataset, by introducing more advanced methods such as machine learning and KD(K-dimensional) tree[10].

References

[1] LIU Y, ZHANG D, LU G, et al. A survey of content-based image retrieval with high level semantics[J]. Pattern recognition, 2007, 40(1): 262-282.

[2] LOWE D G. Distinctive image features from scale invariant key points[J]. International journal of computer vision, 2004, 60(2): 91-110.

[3] MIKOLAJCZYK K, SCHMID C. Indexing based on scale invariant interest points[J]. Proceedings of the 8th International Conference on Computer Vision Vancouver, 2002, 1: 525-531.

[4] ALMEIDA J, TORRES R S, GOLDENSTEIN S. SIFT applied to CBIR, Salesian[J]. Journal on information systems, 2009, 4: 41-48.

[5] GONZALEZ R C, WOODS R E, EDDINS S L. Digital Image Processing[M]. Beijing: Publishing House of Electronics Industry, 2009.

[6] DAVIDLOW G. Object Recognition from Local Scale-Invariant Features[C]. The Proceedings of the Seventh IEEE International Conference

on Computer Vision, IEEE Computer Society Press, Corfu, Greece. 1999: 1150-1157.

[7] BROWN M, LOWE D G. Invariant features from interest point groups[C]. British Machine Vision Conference, BMVC 2002, British Machine Vision Association, Cardiff, Wales, 2002: 656-665.

[8] MESHRAML KIMAYA S, AGARKAR AJAY M. Content based image retrieval systems using SIFT: A survey[J]. SSRG International journal of electronics and communication engineering (SSRG-IJECE), 2015, 2(10): 18-25.

[9] LINDEBERY T. Scale-space theory: A basic tool for analyzing structures at different scales[J]. Journal of applied statistics, 1994, 21(2): 224-270.

[10] LOWE DAVID. Scale invariant feature transform[EB/OL]. [2018-06-15]. http://en.wikipedia.org/wiki/Scale-invariant_feature_transform.

[11] LI Z, LIU Y. An improved texture feature extraction method for tire tread patterns[J]. IScIDE 2013, 2013, 8261: 705-713.

[12] TAMURA H, MORI S, YAMAEAKI J. Texture features corresponding to visual perception[J]. IEEE transactions on systems, man and cybernetics, 1978, 8(6): 460-473.

Chapter 5

Study on Rotation-Invariant Texture Feature Extraction for Tire Pattern Retrieval

5.1 Introduction

In crime scene and traffic accident investigations, tire pattern is considered as one of the most vital clue. Finding the target's tire pattern from the database quickly is very critical[1]. Though many algorithms have been designed for image feature extraction, literature survey shows that there is little work done specifically for tire pattern retrieval.

Texture feature plays a key role in tire pattern retrieval. Chapter 3 describes a new Tamura-based texture feature extraction method for tire pattern, which makes use of the statistical moments of intensity histogram to extract more information from the image. Test results show that this method is effective for tire pattern texture feature description[2]. In this chapter, we will discuss transform-domain texture feature for tire pattern images.

Wavelet transform is a typical image multi-resolution analysis tool, and it has been widely used for texture feature extraction [3,4]. However,

5.1 Introduction

wavelet-based texture feature is sensitive to image rotation[5]. Another drawback of wavelet transform is its translation sensitivity. Therefore wavelet-based texture feature is less robust and affect its application in image retrieval.

In order to overcome these problems, Kingsbury[6] proposed dual tree complex wavelet transform (DT-CWT), which is less sensitive to image direction than wavelet transform. However, it does not take into consideration the rotation of images.

Curvelet transform is a relatively new multi-resolution analyzing tool[7,8]. It performs well in resolving curve and complex texture. Curvelet transform provides more directional information and is hence more suitable for retrieving tire pattern database than wavelet transform which provides only information in four directions[9]. However, similar to wavelet transform, curvelet transform, is also not rotation invariant.

This chapter studies on rotation-invariant texture feature extraction for tire patterns and proposes two different methods. The first method combines Radon transform with multi-scale analysis, referred to as Radon-DTCWT. Rotation of an image by a certain angle leads to a linear shift of its Radon transform coefficient[10,11]. Using this characteristic of Randon transform, the texture features obtained using Radon-DTCWT becomes rotation invariant. Experiment results show that the Radon-DTCWT based method effectively improves the retrieval performance of rotated images significantly.

Another method presented in this chapter is curvelet energy distribution algorithm(CEDA), which extracts the mean and variance of each subband in curvelet transform domain as the texture feature value of an image. After calculating the energy of each subband, CEDA then sorts and cyclically shifts the feature vector, so as to make the largest energy feature value in the first place of the feature vector. This could ensure that the feature vector does not change with image rotation and hence achieves rotation invariance property. Experimental results show that CEDA is very effective in describing tire patterns.

The rest of the chapter is structured as follows: In Section 5.2, Radon-DTCWT is introduced. Section 5.3 describes CEDA in details. Section 5.4 presents experimental results on a set of real-world tire patterns and finally Section 5.5 concludes this chapter.

5.2 Radon-DTCWT Algorithm

5.2.1 Radon transform

The Radon transform of $f(x_1, x_2)$ in R^2 is defined as[12]:

$$R_f(\theta, t) = \iint_{R\,R} f(x_1, x_2) \delta(x_1 \cos\theta + x_2 \sin\theta - t) \mathrm{d}x_1 \mathrm{d}x_2 \tag{5-1}$$

Where θ is the direction parameters, R_f is the integral projection in the direction of each θ, it can be regarded as the simple integration in the new coordinate system. Fig. 5-1 shows the relations.

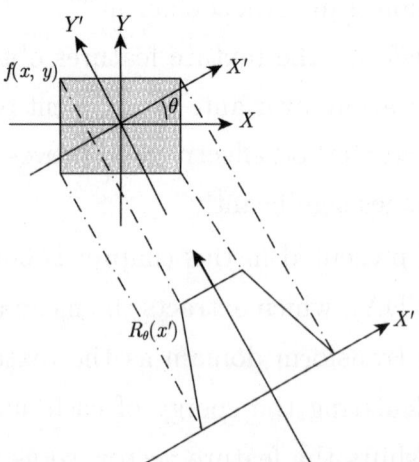

Fig. 5-1 Geometric relationships of Radon transform

5.2 Radon-DTCWT Algorithm

Assuming that the original image is $f_1(x_1, y_1)$, $f_2(x_1, x_2)$ is the image after rotating by $\Delta\theta$. The Radon transform of $f_2(x_1, x_2)$ is:

$$R_{f2}(\theta, t) = \iint_{RR} f(y_1, y_2) \delta[y_1 \cos(\theta - \Delta\theta) + y_2 \sin(\theta - \Delta\theta) - t] dy_1 dy_2$$

$$= R_{f1}[(\theta - \Delta\theta), t] \tag{5-2}$$

It can be inferred from formula (5-1) and formula (5-2) that the translation of the original image is equal to t translation, rotation of original image is equal to θ translation, scaling the image will cause a more complex variation of Radon coefficients.

5.2.2 Translation sensitivity of ridgelet transform

Through Radon transform, we obtain a 1-D sequence for each angle projection. This algorithm projects image to N directions, and each direction has N sub-point, where N is the size of the image. The projection matrix is composed of N directions:

$$R_f = \begin{bmatrix} g_{\theta 1}(1) & g_{\theta 1}(2) & \cdots & g_{\theta 1}(N) \\ g_{\theta 2}(1) & g_{\theta 2}(2) & \cdots & g_{\theta 2}(N) \\ \vdots & \vdots & & \vdots \\ g_{\theta N}(1) & g_{\theta N}(2) & \cdots & g_{\theta N}(N) \end{bmatrix} \tag{5-3}$$

Further, the ridgelet transform is done by performing 1-D DWT on each column in formula (5-3)[13]. The approximate rotation invariant texture feature vector can then be extracted from the energy, variance and other feature value.

Ridgelet function[14] is defined as:

$$\psi_{a,b,\theta} = a^{-\frac{1}{2}} \psi \left(\frac{x_1 \cos\theta + x_2 \sin\theta - b}{a} \right) \tag{5-4}$$

Where $a > 0, a, b, x_1, x_2 \in R, \theta \in [0, \pi]$, and the Ridglet transform of $f(x)$ is defined as:

$$\text{RFT}_f(a, b, \theta) = \int_{R^2} \psi_{a,b,\theta} f(x) \mathrm{d}x \tag{5-5}$$

The continuous wavelet transform of $f(x)$ on R^2 is:

$$W_f(a, b) = \int_{R^2} \psi_{a,b}(x) f(x) \mathrm{d}x \tag{5-6}$$

Where $\psi_{a,b}(x) = a^{-\frac{1}{2}} \psi \left(\dfrac{x-a}{b} \right)$ is the 1-D wavelet function, so that combined with (1), the ridgelet transform can be defined[13] as:

$$\text{RFT}_f(a, b, \theta) = \int_{R^2} \psi_{a,b}(x) R_f(\theta, t) \mathrm{d}t \tag{5-7}$$

The above formula indicates that ridgelet transform can be seen as a special wavelet transform in Radon domain. The problem is that small translation in the coefficients in angle direction occurs when the rotation of the image is converted into cyclic shift of the angle parameters. Fig. 5-2 gives an example on how the Radon domain coefficients of an image are affected by the rotation of the image in space domain.

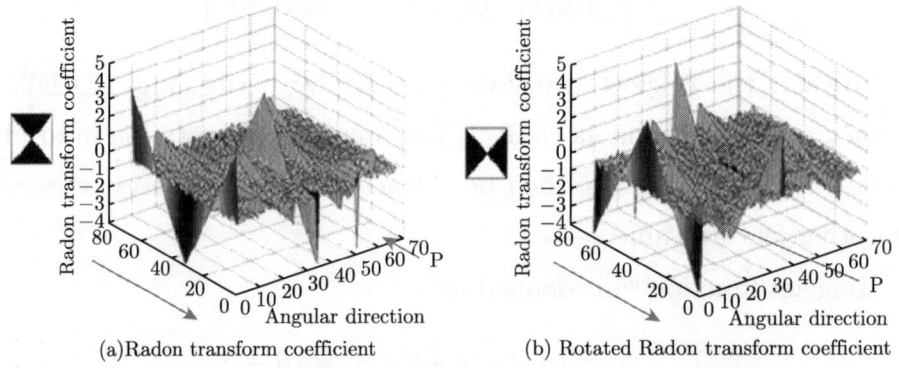

(a) Radon transform coefficient (b) Rotated Radon transform coefficient

Fig. 5-2 Coefficients variation of Radon transform

5.2 Radon-DTCWT Algorithm

It's clear that the peak in the lower right corner in Fig. 5-2(a) is translated to the other side of the coordinates in Fig. 5-2(b). This small translation will result in a big change in its wavelet coefficients as displayed in Fig. 5-3.

Fig. 5-3 reveals that although the sequence only moves to the left by one step, there is a big change in the wavelet coefficient distribution implying that wavelet transform is not translation invariant. The new Radon-DTCWT algorithm uses DT-CWT after Radon transform in order to overcome the defect of ridgelet transform.

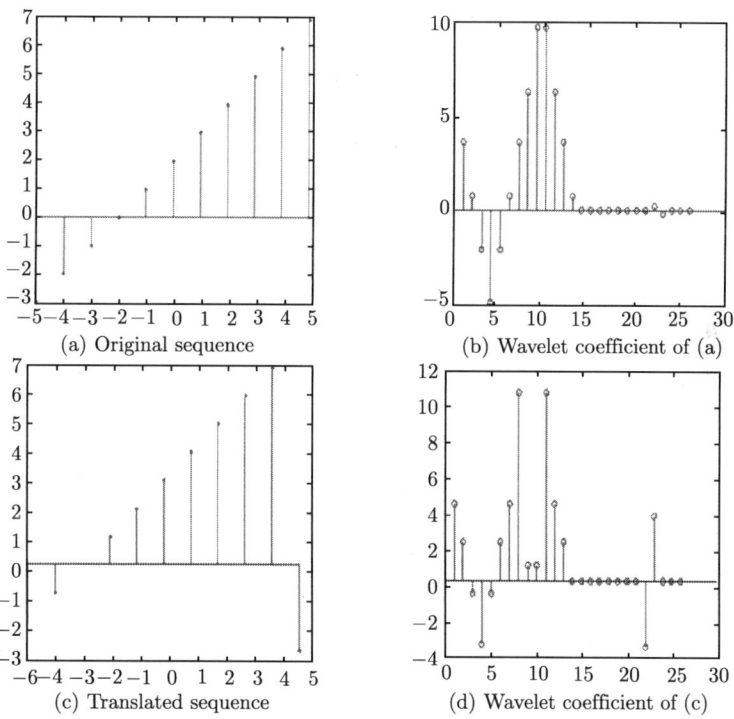

Fig. 5-3 The influence of translation on the wavelet coefficient

The diagrams reveals that although the sequence only moves to the left by one step, there is a huge change in the wavelet coefficient distribution implying that wavelet transform is not translation invariant. The new Radon-DTCWT algorithm performed DT-CWT on Radon transform in order to overcome the short coming of ridgelet transform.

5.2.3 The new Radon-DTCWT algorithm

The new Radon-DTCWT algorithm combines Radon transform and DT-CWT together. DT-CWT not only keeps the good analysis ability of local change in spatial domain, but also has the approximate shift invariance property, less data redundancy and has perfect reconstruction[15,16]. The DT-CWT is defined as[17]:

$$\psi_c(x) = \psi_h(x) + j\psi_g(x) \tag{5-8}$$

Where j is imaginary, ψ_h, ψ_g is orthogonal or biorthogonal real wavelet.

In order to realize DT-CWT, the filter should meet the following condition.

$$\begin{cases} \varphi_h(x) = \sqrt{2}\sum_n h_0(n)\varphi_h(2x-n) \\ \psi_h(x) = \sqrt{2}\sum_n h_1(n)\varphi_h(2x-n) \\ \tilde{\varphi}_h(x) = \sqrt{2}\sum_n \tilde{h}_0(n)\tilde{\varphi}_h(2x-n) \\ \tilde{\psi}_h(x) = \sqrt{2}\sum_n \tilde{h}_1(n)\tilde{\varphi}_h(2x-n) \end{cases}$$

$$\begin{cases} \varphi_g(x) = \sqrt{2}\sum_n g_0(n)\varphi_g(2x-n) \\ \psi_g(x) = \sqrt{2}\sum_n g_1(n)\varphi_g(2x-n) \\ \tilde{\varphi}_g(x) = \sqrt{2}\sum_n \tilde{g}_0(n)\tilde{\varphi}_g(2x-n) \\ \tilde{\psi}_g(x) = \sqrt{2}\sum_n \tilde{g}_1(n)\tilde{\varphi}_g(2x-n) \end{cases} \tag{5-9}$$

5.2 Radon-DTCWT Algorithm

Where φ_h, $\tilde{\varphi}_h$ and $\tilde{\psi}_h$, ψ_h are biorthogonal dual scaling function and dual wavelet, h_0, $\tilde{h}_0$, g_0, $\tilde{g}_0$ and h_1, $\tilde{h}_1$, g_1, $\tilde{g}_1$ are the corresponding low-pass and high-pass filters.

Fig. 5-4 shows a one-dimensional signal processing diagram of dual tree complex wavelet decomposition. It consists of two parallel real wavelet tree. Tree A is the real component of wavelet coefficients and tree B is the imaginary part.

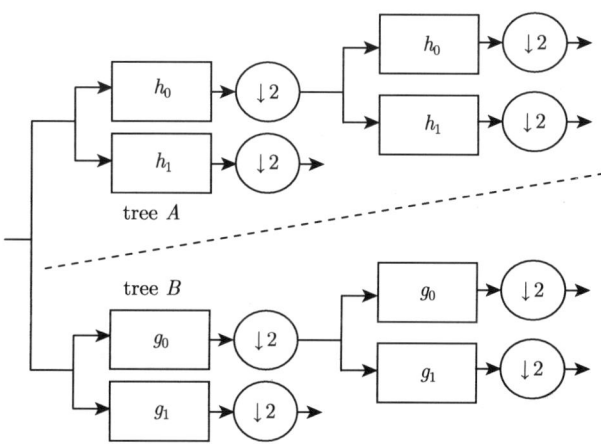

Fig. 5-4 DT-CWT analysis filter bank

It has been proved in [6] that if $g_0(n) = h_0(n - 0.5)$, ψ_h and $j\psi_g$ are Hilbert transform pairs. Low pass filter of tree A and tree B achieve the half sampling delay, which makes DT-CWT approximate shift invariance. And this characteristic helps to overcome the problems of wavelet transforming after Radon transform.

The DT-CWT for $f(x) \in R^2$ is:

$$< f, \psi_c > = < f, \psi_h > + j < f, \psi_g > \qquad (5\text{-}10)$$

The proposed Radon-DTCWT algorithm uses one-dimensional DT-CWT on Radon domain and is defined as:

$$\text{DTRFT}_f = <R_f, \psi_c> = <R_f, \psi_h> + j <R_f, \psi_g>$$
$$= \int_{R^2} \psi_c(x) R_f(\theta, t) dt + j \int_{R^2} \psi_g(x) R_f(\theta, t) dt \qquad (5\text{-}11)$$

It can be seen from formula (5-11) that the Radon-DTCWT method and DT-CWT can be combined by Radon transform. And Fig. 5-5 shows the flow chart of the new Radon-DTCWT algorithm.

The new Radon-DTCWT algorithm is described as following:

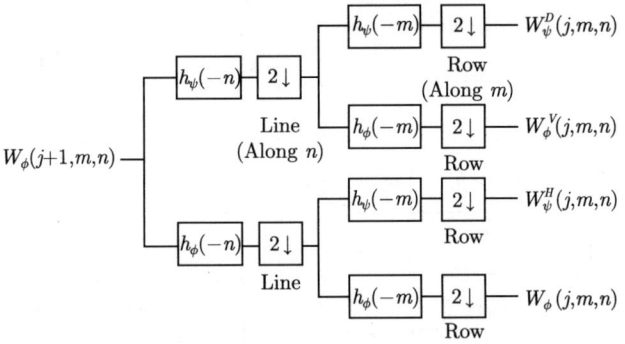

Fig. 5-5   Flow chart of the new Radon-DTCWT algorithm

(1) Perform Radon transform on the original image. $(g_{\theta i}(1), g_{\theta i}(2), \cdots, g_{\theta i}(N))$ is the projection sequence of $f(x, y)$ under an arbitrary angle. And R_f is the projection matrix composes of all the angle projection in a matrix form.

(2) The 3-level DT-CWT is performed on each row in R_f, which consists of 9 high frequency subbands and 1 low frequency subband.

(3) Calculate the mean (M), variance (σ) and energy (E) of each subband to obtain the feature vector. The mean, variance and energy of level i are:

$$M_i = \frac{1}{MN} \sum_{x=1}^{M} \sum_{y=1}^{N} |I_i(x, y)| \qquad (5\text{-}12)$$

$$\sigma_i = \sqrt{\frac{1}{MN} \sum_{x=1}^{M} \sum_{y=1}^{N} (I_i(x, y) - M_i)^2} \qquad (5\text{-}13)$$

5.3 Curvelet Energy Distribution Algorithm

$$E_i = \frac{1}{MN} \sum_{x=1}^{M} \sum_{y=1}^{N} I_i^2(x,y) \qquad (5\text{-}14)$$

The feature vector is:

$$f = (M_1, \sigma_1, E_1, M_2, \sigma_2, E_2, \cdots, M_{10}, \sigma_{10}, E_{10})$$

(4) Normalize the feature vector and calculate the Euclidean distance between two images. The distance is used to measure the similarity between the two images and finally the images with the smallest distances are retrieved.

5.3 Curvelet Energy Distribution Algorithm

5.3.1 Curvelet transform of tire pattern image

Another algorithm based on curvelet transform is also proposed to alleviate the influence of image rotation in image retrieval applications.

In[7], curvelet transform of an image $f[t_1, t_2]$, $0 \leqslant t_1 \leqslant t_2 < n$ is defined as:

$$c^D = \sum_{0 \leqslant t_1 \leqslant t_2 < n} f[t_1, t_2] \overline{\phi_{j,k,l}^D[t_1, t_2]} \qquad (5\text{-}15)$$

Where $\phi_{j,k,l}^D$ is the discrete Curvelet waveform. $[t_1, t_2]$ is a pixel of input image, where t_1 represents its abscissa, t_2 represents its ordinate. c^D is coefficient of Curvelet transform.

Fig. 5-6 shows the Curvelet transform frequency map. According to formula (5-11), the direction of the tire pattern corresponds to a particular subband's energy distribution shape. Referring to Fig. 5-6, when the image has more vertical texture, energy is concentrated in subband No.1 and No.2 at level 1. Similarly, energy is also concentrated in subband No.2 and No.3 at level 2.

Using formula (5-11) to transform an example of a tire image, a band diagram is shown in Fig. 5-7.

The texture of the image in Fig 5-7(a) is mainly composed of vertical direction. It is observed that the energy of most coefficients are concentrated in the vertical subbands as shown in Fig.5-7(b). Therefore, by computing he energy distribution of each subband, the direction in an image can be determined.

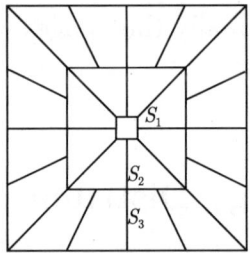

Fig. 5-6　Frequency map of curvelet transform

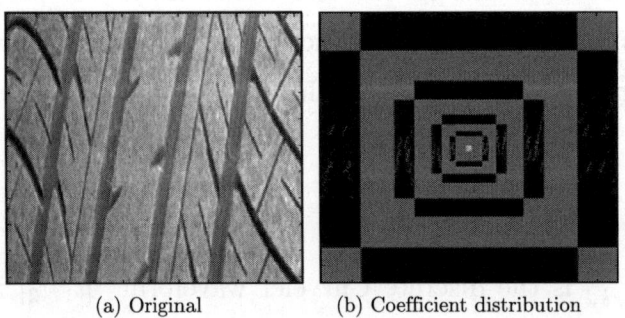

(a) Original　　　　(b) Coefficient distribution

Fig. 5-7　Curvelet transform of a tire pattern

5.3.2　Direction characteristics of tire pattern images

According to the percentage of high frequency subband of transformed image, the tire pattern image can be classified into four categories. They are vertical, horizontal, diagonal and irregular types. An image is classified as vertical type when the energy of the vertical subband is the

5.3 Curvelet Energy Distribution Algorithm

largest. Classification of horizontal type is done similarly. The diagonal type refers to those tire with energy of vertical and horizontal ratio being similar and having largest diagonal subband energy. The irregular type is the remainder which does not fit into the above three categories. Fig. 5-8 shows the four different kinds of tire images.

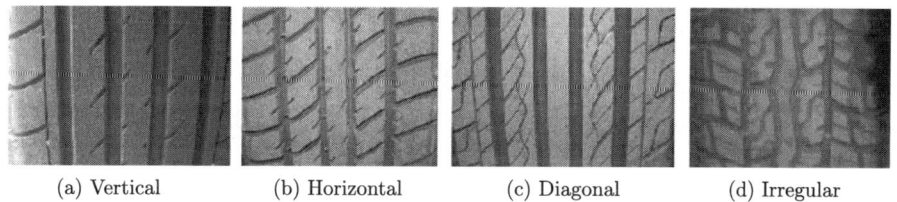

(a) Vertical (b) Horizontal (c) Diagonal (d) Irregular

Fig. 5-8 Different types of tire pattern

Table 5-1 shows the energy distribution of four different kinds of images at level 1 of curvelet transform, the percentage can be computed by calculating the energy distribution of high frequency subband coefficients. Table 5-2 provides the energy distribution of the four images at level 2 of curvelet transform.

It can be seen from Table 5-1 and Table 5-2 that the energy of vertical type image concentrated in subband No.1 and No.2 at level 1. And at level 2, the energy is concentrated in subband No.3. The energy of horizontal type image is concentrated in subband No.3 and No.4 at level 1. At level 2, the energy is concentrated in subband No.6 and No.7.

Table 5-1 **Energy distribution of level 1**

Subband	Energy distribution/%			
	vertical	horizontal	diagonal	irregular
1	43.40	6.88	33.9	21.00
2	31.11	10.12	6.34	30.05
3	14.09	24.90	20.80	28.41
4	11.40	58.10	38.96	20.55

Table 5-2 Energy distribution of level 2

Subband	Energy distribution/%			
	vertical	horizontal	diagonal	irregular
1	4.13	8.19	21.85	3.17
2	7.94	10.76	17.39	19.08
3	33.81	9.72	7.97	21.17
4	14.06	7.26	2.33	3.58
5	10.18	8.19	3.63	3.34
6	16.17	21.03	11.03	25.90
7	9.65	27.31	14.08	20.53
8	4.06	7.54	21.73	3.17

Therefore, the type of tire pattern image can be judged by the largest concentration of subband energy. When an image rotation occurs, the concentration of the energy in the subband will also be displaced along the rotational path. This displacement will also affect the retrieval precision. To overcome this problem, in our proposed CEDA, we reconstruct the feature vector to eliminate the influence caused by rotation.

5.3.3 Implementation of Curvelet energy distribution algorithm

When a vertical type image is rotated by 90°, the rotated image will change to horizontal type. Fig. 5-9 shows the same image with different rotation angle. It is observed that the rotation caused a very big change in energy distribution, Table 5-3 shows the change of energy distribution.

The texture feature is defined as a 52-dimensional feature vector that includes: mean and variance of No.1~No.4 subband at level 1, mean and variance of No.1~No.8 subband at level 2, and mean and

5.3 Curvelet Energy Distribution Algorithm

variance in low frequency subband.

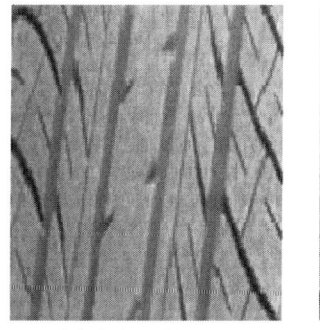 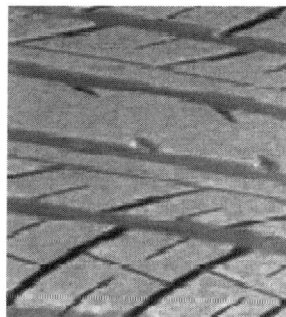

(a) Original image   (b) Rotated image

Fig. 5-9   Same image with different angle

Table 5-3   Energy distribution

Subband	Energy distribution/%	
	(a)	(b)
1	59.53	1.52
2	37.58	1.73
3	1.34	60.89
4	1.55	35.86

Our proposed CEDA can be described as follows:

(1) Perform 2-level curvelet transform on the tire pattern image.

(2) Calculate the mean and variance of 13 subbands as feature vector.

(3) Calculate energy distribution of each level, choose the highest energy subband, and make this subband as the reference subband.

(4) Circular left shift whole original feature vector until the feature value of reference subband in the head.

This will allow the highest energy subband in the first and this reference subband will not change with image rotation.

Through the above process, no matter how the image rotated, the corresponding feature value of reference subband will always be first in feature vector line. In addition, the relationship and arrangement between the components will not be disrupted, which keeps the singularity of the feature vector. This method eliminates the influence caused by rotation. Fig. 5-10 shows the flow of CEDA.

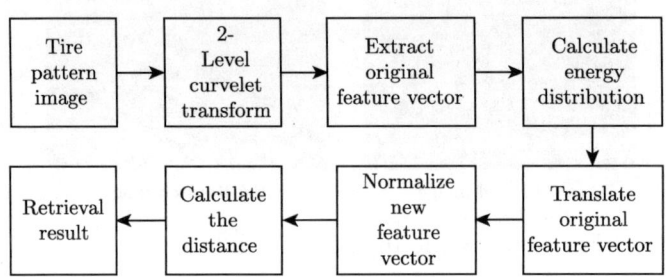

Fig. 5-10 Flow chart of the CEDA

5.4 Experiment Results

A set of experiments were performed on a tire tread pattern dataset from a public security criminal investigation database. The tire dataset contains 200 images in 40 categories with 5 similar images in each category. The wavelet transform method, curvelet transform method as well as DT-CWT method were used to compare with the proposed Radon-DTCWT algorithm and CEDA.

In order to compare the performances, we used precision to k curve to evaluate the performance of each method. The precision is defined as:

$$\text{precision} = \frac{s}{k} \tag{5-16}$$

Where s is the number of relevant images retrieved, k is the total number of images returned.

By retrieving all tire pattern images in tire pattern database, the average precision is computed. The following shows the retrieval comparison as in Fig. 5-11.

5.4 Experiment Results

Fig. 5-11(a) is the image query, and the performance of different method is compared. Fig. 5-11(b)~Fig. 5-11(f) show the retrieved result of 5 different algorithms, where T (TRUE) represent result is the actual related image and F otherwise. The result in Fig. 5-11(b) shows

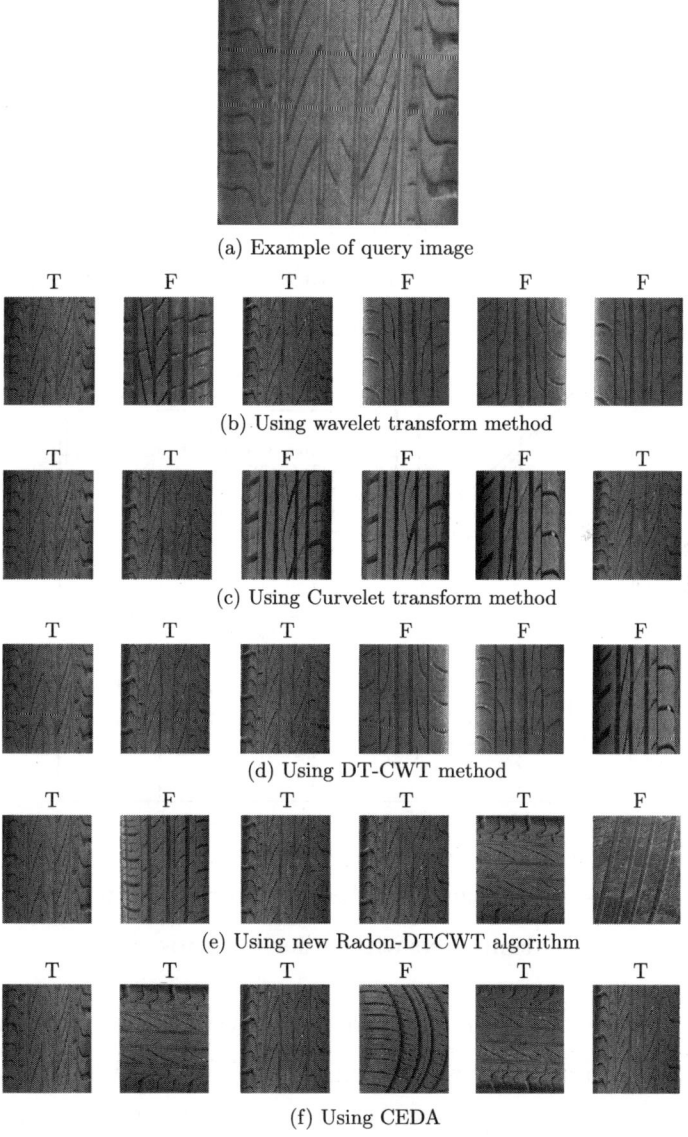

Fig. 5-11 Retrieval results

that the algorithm based on wavelet transform[7] has worst performance, only 2 related image returned. The reason is that the other 4 related images have different direction compared to the query image. The wavelet transform algorithm performance is obviously influenced by image rotation. The algorithm based on Curvelet transform and DT-CWT in Fig. 5-11(c) and Fig. 5-11(d) do not perform well for rotated image. In fact, the first three methods did not return the rotated image at all.

Fig. 5-11(e) and Fig. 5-11(f) show better results because the features used are almost rotation invariance. The Radon-DTCWT algorithm and CEDA both returned rotated image.

The precision of the various methods are shown in Fig. 5-12, where k is the total number of returned images.

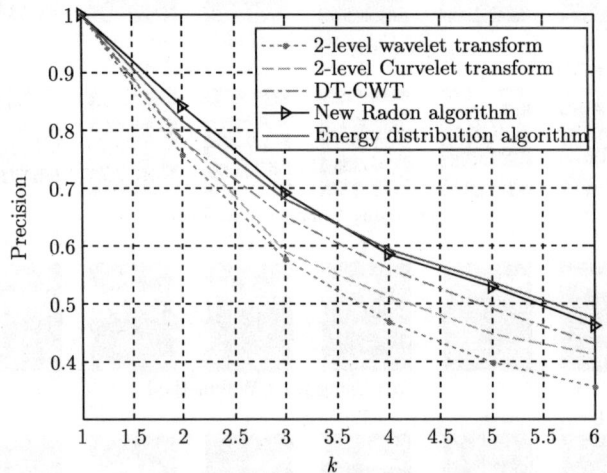

Fig. 5-12 Retrieval results of the proposed method compared with other methods

Fig. 5-12 shows that the new Radon-DTCWT algorithm and CEDA perform better than other algorithms. The new methods improved the precision of tire texture database by 47.25% and 48% respectively. This is because the methods are rotation invariance, and also overcome the problem of translation in the wavelet transform domain.

It can be seen that wavelet transform method is least time consuming while Radon-DTCWT method cost little more time which is still practical given the significant higher precision.Table 5-4 shows the average time on each method.

Table 5-4   Average time cost

Method	Wavelet transform method	Curvelet transform method	DT-CWT	Radon-DTCWT method	CEDA
Time cost/s	1.25	2.61	1.56	3.45	2.23

5.5 Conclusions

This chapter presented two rotation invariant texture feature extraction methods. In Radon-DTCWT method, we combined Radon transform and DT-CWT to extract texture feature that is rotation invariant. The CEDA method calculated the energy of each subband in curvelet transform domain, and then sorted and circularly shifted the feature vector, so that the feature vector does not change with image rotation. Our experiment results demonstrated the good performance of both Radon-DTCWT and CEDA in tire pattern retrieval.

References

[1] LIU Y, ZHANG D S, LU G J. A survey of content-based image retrieval with high level semantics[J]. Pattern recognition, 2008, 40(1): 262-282.

[2] LI Z, LIU Y, LI D X. A new texture feature extraction method for image retrieval[C]. 2013 Fourth International Conference on Intelligent Control

and Information Processing, Beijing, China, 2013: 482-486.

[3] MALLAT S G. A theory for multiresolution signal decomposition: the wavelet representation[J]. IEEE transactions on pattern analysis and machine intelligence, 1989, 11(7): 674-693.

[4] VETTERLI M. Wavelets, approximation and compression[J]. IEEE signal processing magazine, 2001, 18(5): 59-73.

[5] AN Z Y, ZHAO S, WANG X H. Content-based image retrieval based on the multi-scale radon transform[J]. Acta photonica sinica, 2007, 36(6): 1176-1180.

[6] KINGSBURY N G. Complex wavelets for shift invariant analysis and filtering of signals[J]. Applied & computational harmonic analysis, 2000, 10(3): 234-253.

[7] CANDS E J, DONOHO D L. Continuous curvelet transform: II. Discretization and frames[J]. Applied & computational harmonic analysis, 2005, 19(2): 198-222.

[8] DONOHO D L, DUNCAN M R. Digital curvelet transform: strategy, implementation and experiments[J]. Proceedings of SPIE-the international society for optical engineering, 2000, 4056: 12-29.

[9] PATIL S, TALBAR S. Multiresolution analysis using complex wavelet and Curvelet features for content based image retrieval[J]. International journal of computer applications, 2012, 47(17): 6-10.

[10] AN Z Y, ZENG Z Y. Content-based image retrieval based on wavelet transform and radon transform[C]. Proceeding of 2nd IEEE Conference on Industrial Electronics and Applications, Shenzhen, China, 2007: 1878-1881.

[11] KOUROSH J K, HAMID S Z. rotation-invariant multiresolution texture analysis using radon and wavelet transform[J]. IEEE transactions on image processing, 2005, 14(6): 783-794.

[12] DEANS S R. The Radon Transform and Some of Its Applications[M]. New York: Wiley, 1983.

[13] CANDS E J. Ridgelets: Theory and Applications[D]. USA: Department of Statistics, Stanford University, 1998.

[14] DONOHO D L. Orthonormal ridgelets and linear singularities[D]. USA: Department of Statistics, Stanford University , 1998.

[15] JIAO L C, TAN S. Development and prospect of image multiscale geometric analysis[J]. Acta photonica sinica, 2003, 31(12A): 1975-1981.

[16] KINGSBURY N G. The dual-tree complex wavelet transform: A new efficient tool for image restoration and enhancement[C]. Signal Processing Conference, IEEE, Quebec city, Canada, 2015: 1-4.

[17] KINGSBURY N G. A dual-tree complex wavelet transform with improved orthogonality and symmetry properties[C]. IEEE International Conference on Image Processing, Vancouver, Canada, 2000, 2: 375-378.

Chapter 6

HOG-TT: A Robust HOG-Based Texture Feature Extraction Method Making Use of Texture Tendency in Tread Pattern Images

6.1 Introduction

Due to the lack of standard test bed in this special field, not much work has been done in texture feature extraction from tread pattern images and existing algorithms mostly are designed based on classical texture features with little modifications[1-4]. For instance, in[1], curvelet transform is first applied onto tread pattern image, then mean and variance are calculated from each subband in curvelet domain to form the texture feature vector, which is cyclically shifted till the statistics of the subband with most energy comes to the first position. The texture feature obtained is rotation-invariant. In [2], the algorithm combines Tamura feature with statistics such as mean, standard deviation and smoothness obtained from the histogram of intensity to describe tread pattern images.

6.1 Introduction

These algorithms, though have brought improvement in tread pattern description to certain extend, are not designed based on the inherent characteristics of tread patterns. Natural texture images such as grass, pebble, generally display similarity in local structure but the internal texture directions are chaotic. Differently, tread pattern image demonstrates obvious texture direction, which is robust to scaling, rotation, illumination changes and noise[1].

Histogram of oriented gradient (HOG) feature[5] describes the distribution of local intensity change in terms of gradient direction and is suitable for texture structure representation. It has good robustness to illumination and scale changes but is sensitive to the rotation transformation which is common in tread pattern image database. In this chapter, making use of the inherent texture tendency in tread pattern image, a novel HOG-based texture feature descriptor named HOG-TT is proposed, which not only inherits the illumination and scale invariant property of HOG, but also overcomes the defect of HOG in being rotation-sensitive by making two major changes.

(1) Circular rings of different radius are defined as cells. In this way, the same group of pixels is contained in a cell no matter how the image rotates.

(2) Texture tendency of the tread pattern image is detected and all the cell feature vectors are aligned to it. The cell feature vector are normalized and concatenated to construct the HOG-TT feature. Experimental results prove that HOG-TT outperforms other methods in describing tread pattern image.

The rest of this chapter is organized as following: Section 6.2 describes the proposed HOG-TT algorithm in details, Section 6.3 provides experimental results and Section 6.4 concludes this chapter.

6.2 Description of HOG-TT

6.2.1 HOG descriptor

Classical HOG feature extraction mainly includes two stages:

1. Histogram extraction of oriented gradient

In this stage, the magnitude and direction of gradient are extracted from each pixel in the image, and these are used to generate the gradient magnitude histogram in terms of gradient direction to obtain the representation vector of image texture. For image $I(i,j)$, the derivatives along direction i,j, at pixel (i,j), the gradient magnitude $G(i,j)$ and direction $\alpha_0(i,j)$ are respectively calculated as follows:

$$G_i(i,j) = I(i+1,j) - I(i-1,j) \tag{6-1}$$

$$G_j(i,j) = I(i,j+1) - I(i,j-1) \tag{6-2}$$

$$G(i,j) = \sqrt{G_i(i,j)^2 + G_j(i,j)^2} \tag{6-3}$$

$$\alpha_0(i,j) = \tan^{-1}\left[\frac{G_j(i,j)}{G_i(i,j)}\right], \alpha_0 \in \left[-\frac{\pi}{2}, \frac{\pi}{2}\right] \tag{6-4}$$

where $G_i(i,j)$ and $G_j(i,j)$ are the derivative along horizontal and vertical direction at pixel (i,j), respectively.

2. Construction of HOG descriptor

In this stage, HOG descriptor is constructed based on the image gradient. Firstly, the whole image is divided into cells of size 8×8. The gradient direction range $[-\pi/2, \pi/2]$ is uniformly quantized into 9 direction intervals (bins). In each cell, the gradient histogram of all the pixels in the cell is calculated in terms of direction bin to obtain a feature vector of length 9. Then, 4 adjacent cells gather into a block and

6.2 Description of HOG-TT

the related feature vectors are concatenated to form a vector of length 36. Finally, scanning the image block-by-block, the HOG feature of image is constructed by concatenating the 36-D vectors of all blocks. To make it robust to illumination changes, the resulted HOG feature is further normalized.

6.2.2 HOG-TT

HOG descriptor has strong representation ability of local image structure. However, it is sensitive to rotation transformation and this limits its use in other fields. This section presents a so-called HOG-TT algorithm specially designed for tread pattern image which overcomes the disadvantage of HOG and produces texture feature robust not only to illumination and scale changes, but also to rotation transformation. The algorithm consists mainly of four steps.

(1) Calculating the gradient magnitude and direction of each pixel in an image.

(2) Defining circular cells and calculating cell feature vectors (CFV).

(3) Detecting texture tendency and aligning all CFVs.

(4) Normalizing CFVs and concatenating them to construct the HOG-TT feature.

1. Defining circular cell and calculating cell feature vector

In order to reserve the content in every cell, we design circular cells instead of squares as in conventional HOG descriptor. Taking the center of the image as the center, circular cells are defined with radius as , while is the radius of the maximum inscribed circle. It can be seen that points 1, 2, 3 on the tread in Fig. 6-1(a), remain in same cell as in Fig. 6-1(b).

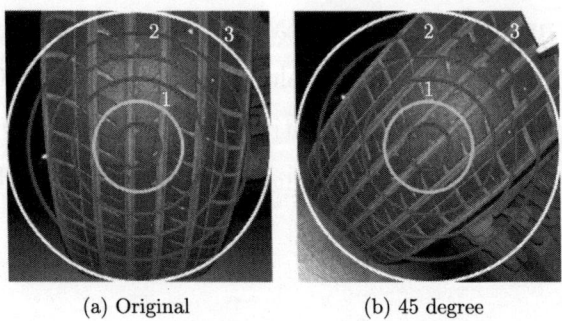

(a) Original   (b) 45 degree

Fig. 6-1   Circular cells

Then, HOG is calculated with the gradient magnitude and direction of each pixel in a cell obtained using formula (6-1)~ formula (6-4).

Different from conventional HOG that defines the gradient direction interval to be $[-\pi/2, \pi/2]$, in HOG-TT, the gradient direction is mapped from $[-\pi/2, \pi/2]$ to $[0, 2\pi]$, for easier matching with the shooting angle of the picture.

$$\alpha(i,j) = \begin{cases} \alpha_0 & G_i \geqslant 0, G_j \geqslant 0 \\ \alpha_0 + \pi & G_i < 0 \\ \alpha_0 + 2\pi & G_i \geqslant 0, G_j < 0 \end{cases}, \text{ where } \alpha_0 \in \left[-\frac{\pi}{2}, \frac{\pi}{2}\right] \quad (6\text{-}5)$$

In the formula (6-5), $\alpha(i,j)$ and α_0 are the gradient direction at location (i,j) for interval for interval $[0, 2\pi]$ and $[-\pi/2, \pi/2]$ respectively. G_i and G_j are the derivatives at location (i,j) along horizontal and vertical direction, respectively.

Then, the gradient direction range $[0, 2\pi]$ is uniformly quantized into 30 direction intervals (bins), that is, $bin\_k = 30$. The number 30 is set based on experimental statistics (given in Section 6.3.1). Thus, we can obtain a 30-D cell feature vector (CFV) for each of the cells, expressed as,

$$\begin{aligned} C_r &= \{c_r(1), c_r(2), \cdots, c_r(k), \cdots, c_r(30)\} \\ r &= 1, 2, 3, \cdots, R \end{aligned} \quad (6\text{-}6)$$

6.2 Description of HOG-TT

with $c_r(k)$ being the component in C_r with directional interval bin_$k = k$.

2. Detecting texture tendency and aligning cell feature vectors

Adding up all the R CFVs together, a 30-D global feature vector (GFV) is obtained as following,

$$G = \{g_1, g_2, \cdots, g_k, \cdots, g_{30}\}, k = 1, 2, \cdots, 30$$

$$g_k = \sum_{r=1}^{R} c_r(k) \qquad (6\text{-}7)$$

Where $c_r(k)$ is the component in C_r with directional interval bin_$k = k$.

Fig. 6-2 gives examples of tire pattern images taken at different shooting conditions. Table 6-1 gives the GFV of the images in Fig. 6-2. In the GFV, the number marked in gray is the dominant component with maximum gradient magnitude, the number marked in black is the

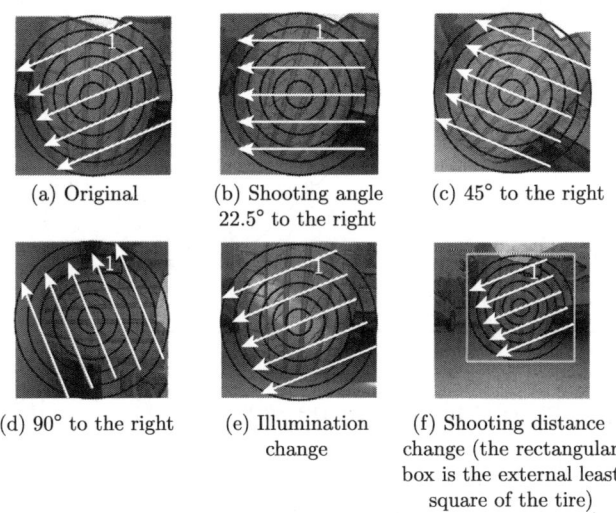

(a) Original (b) Shooting angle 22.5° to the right (c) 45° to the right

(d) 90° to the right (e) Illumination change (f) Shooting distance change (the rectangular box is the external least square of the tire)

Fig. 6-2   Tread pattern image for same tire under different shooting conditions

(circular rings in the image are the cells, and the arrows show the texture tendency)

Table 6-1 GFV of the images in Fig. 6-2

	Shooting condition	(a)	(b)	(c)	(d)	(e)	(f)
	1	5.75	5.29	3.97	5.72	4.61	5.47
	2	4.91	4.99	4.11	5.58	3.57	5.07
	3	6.04	3.23	4.02	5.11	6.00	5.86
	4	7.43	8.57	3.01	5.82	9.62	7.83
	5	9.55	9.14	6.96	5.97	13.0	9.21
	6	5.49	9.62	8.72	4.04	4.94	5.69
	7	5.7	5.43	10.7	6.12	4.50	5.51
	8	5.19	5.05	6.71	6.98	3.67	5.38
$c_r(k)$	9	5.47	4.39	5.02	9.75	4.30	5.27
	10	4.77	5.98	5.16	5.24	3.55	4.84
	11	9.79	4.26	5.54	6.01	13.7	9.53
	12	7.21	10.1	2.93	5.26	8.58	7.54
	13	5.84	8.21	12.3	5.59	5.82	5.72
	14	5.49	5.02	9.99	4.12	5.3	5.68
	15	5.91	5.39	6.54	9.82	4.99	5.68
	16	5.46	5.33	4.32	8.87	3.84	5.72

2nd dominant component. It can be seen that the 'position' k_m of the dominant component shifts with the change in the shooting angle, and the relationship between the shifting amount Δk and the change in the shooting angle $\Delta \alpha$ is,

$$\Delta \alpha = \Delta k \cdot \frac{2\pi}{\text{bin\_}k} \tag{6-8}$$

$$k_m = \arg\max_{k}\{g(k), k = 1, 2, \cdots, 30\} \tag{6-9}$$

where k_m is the directional bin of the dominant component in G.

The 'position' k_m (directional interval) of the dominant component in the GFV determines the texture tendency in the tread image. The arrows in Fig. 6-2 are for demonstration purpose with the direction being the left endpoint of k_m. Under illumination and scale changes, the texture tendency remains unchanged. It can be stated that the texture tendency of tread image is robust to rotation, illumination and scale changes.

Based on the relationship between the texture tendency and the shooting angle, we propose to align all the CFVs to the texture tendency by cyclically shifting each CFV by $k_m - 1$ to the left.

$$C'_r = f_{\text{CircleShift}}(C_r, k_m - 1) \tag{6-10}$$

3. Normalization and concatenation

Then, each of aligned cell feature vector C'_r is normalized using L1-norm. Finally, all the R normalized cell feature vectors $C_r^N (r = 1, 2, \cdots, R)$ are concatenated to construct the final HOG-TT feature with $R \cdot 30$ dimension.

6.3 Experimental Results

In our experiments, the dataset 'CIIP-Tread Data' is used, which contains 5,100 tread pattern images in 102 classes. This is a self-built dataset by Center for Image and Information Processing (CIIP), Xi'an University of Posts and Telecommunication collaborating with local public security organization. Each class contains 50 tread pattern images obtained under different shooting conditions (with changes in illumination, scale and shooting angles). Examples can be seen in Fig.6-1 and Fig. 6-2.

To test the performance of HOG-TT, LIBSVM classifier (with RBF: radical basis function) is trained for tread pattern classification, with 4/5 of the images used for training and 1/5 for testing. The program is run under MATLAB 2014, with PC setting as Windows 7 Ultimate, Core i5-4258U @ 2.40GHz and NVIDIA GeForce GT 820M.

The performance evaluation parameters used include: classification accuracy (CA) and algorithm running time (ART) as defined in formula (6-11) and formula (6-12),

$$\text{CA} = \left(\frac{N}{M}\right) \times 100\% \tag{6-11}$$

where M is the number of samples to be classified and N the number of correct classifications.

$$T = T_{\text{Fea}} + T_{\text{Tra}} \tag{6-12}$$

where $T_{\text{Fea}}, T_{\text{Tra}}$ represent the amount of time used for feature extraction, for training SVM classifier, respectively.

1. Determining the number of direction intervals

In HOG-TT, the larger the value of bin_k, the higher the feature dimension is. Fig. 6-3 explains how CA changes with the value of bin_k. It is found that the value of CA increases with the increase of bin_k at first, and converges when bin_k reaches 30. In other words, afterwards, further increase in the value of bin_k only results in higher feature dimension, but no further improvement in classification performance. Hence, bin_k is set to 30. That is, the gradient direction range $[0, 2\pi]$ is uniformly quantized into 30 direction intervals (bins).

6.3 Experimental Results

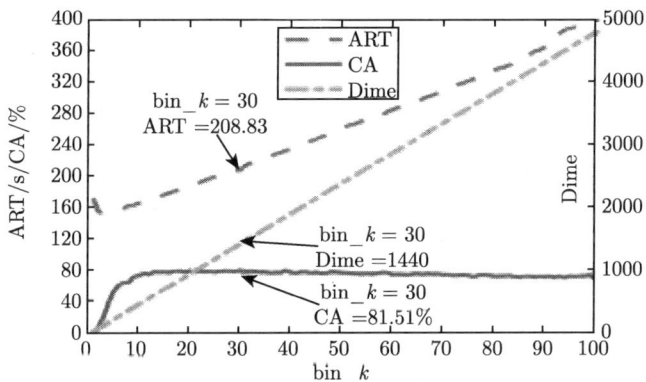

Fig. 6-3 Classification performance value of bin_k

2. Choosing the best normalization method

As described in Section 6.2.2, each of the aligned cell feature vector is normalized before they are concatenated to form the final HOG-TT feature. Table 6-2 compares the classification results with HOG-TT obtained using different normalization methods including L1-norm, L1-sqrt and L2-norm. It is shown that L1-norm outperforms the other two. Hence, L1-norm is chosen to be used in HOG-TT.

Table 6-2 Comparison of different normalization methods

Normalization methods	Classification accuracy (CA)
L1-norm	81.61%
L1-sqrt	78.36%
L2-norm	75.17%
No-norm	59.82%

3. Classification performance comparison

In this experiment, different texture features are used to train LIBSVM classifier for tread pattern classification, including HOG-TT, HOG by Dalal[5], DWT-based texture feature[6], curvelet domain energy distribution algorithm (CEDA)[1], compressed histogram of oriented gradients (CHOG) [7]. In addition, CNNs (convolutional neural networks)[8] trained by Alexnet is also tested.

Fig. 6-4 compares CA of different algorithms tested on different subsets of the CIIP-Treat Data. It can be seen that HOG-TT provides the best performance among all, with its performance close to that of CNNs and CHOG, but clearly better than HOG. For example, for the 5,000 datasets, the CA value of HOG-TT is 81.51%, slightly higher than that of CNNs (80.36%) and CHOG (78.93%), and is 13.21% higher than that of HOG (68.30%).

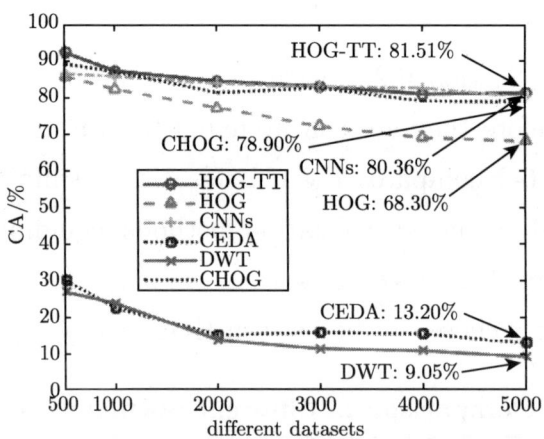

Fig.6-4　Classification performance comparison

Table 6-3 compares the feature dimension (DIME), algorithm running time (ART) of different features tested. Obviously HOG-TT takes less running time than HOG, CHOG and CNNs. DWT and CEDA though have less complexity in computation but their classification performance ranks far behind others.

Table 6-3　Computational load of different texture features

Parameter	HOG-TT	CHOG	HOG	CNNs	CEDA	DWT
DIME	1440	1800	4356	4096	54	14
ART/s	208.83	463.96	402.65	899.22	79.74	29.65

From the above experimental results, it can be concluded that HOG-TT is effective in describing texture feature of tread pattern image and it is robust under different conditions such as illumination, scale and shooting angle changes. In our experiments, CNNs did not demonstrate any advantage over HOG-TT. A possible reason could be that the scale of the test dataset is not very large. This will be further explored in our future work.

6.4 Conclusions

Making use of the inherent texture tendency in tread pattern image, this chapter proposed a novel HOG-based texture feature extraction algorithm HOG-TT, which is robust not only to illumination and scale changes, but also to rotation transformation. HOG-TT makes two major changes compared with HOG descriptor, to overcome its drawback of not being rotation-invariant. ① Defining circular cells instead of square cells so that the pixels in each cell remain the same under rotation; ② Each cell feature vector is aligned to the texture tendency detected in the image. The HOG-TT feature was used to train SVM classifier for tread pattern classification and experimental results proved the effectiveness of HOG-TT in describing tread pattern images.

References

[1] LIU Y, YAN H Y, LIM K P. Study on rotation-invariant texture feature extraction for tire pattern retrieval[J]. Multidimensional systems and signal processing, 2015, 28(2): 757-770.

[2] LIU Y, LI Z, GAO Z M. An improved texture feature extraction method for tire tread pattern[J]. Lecture notes in computer science, 2013, 8261:

705-713.

[3] AI L M, GUO C. Tire tread pattern recognition based on composite feature extraction and hierarchical support vector machine[J]. Computer engineering and application, 2013, 49(20): 179-182.

[4] WANG S, LIU Y. An improved sift feature extraction method for tire tread patterns retrieval[C]. 7th International Symposium on Computational Intelligence and Design(ISCID), Hangzhou, China, 2014: 539-543.

[5] DALAL N, TRIGGS B. Histograms of oriented gradients for human detection [C]. 2005 IEEE Computer Society Conference on Computer Vision and Pattern Recognition(CVPR), Diego, USA, 2005: 886-893.

[6] HEIL C E, WALNUT D F. Continuous and discrete wavelet transforms[J]. SIAM review, 1989, 31(4): 628-666.

[7] CHANDRASEKHAR V, TAKACS G, CHEN D. CHOG: Compressed histogram of gradients A low bit-rate feature descriptor[C]. IEEE Computer Society Conference on Computer Vision and Pattern Recognition Workshops, Miami, USA, 2009: 2504-2511.

[8] YUAN Z W, ZHANG J. Feature extraction and image retrieval based on alexnet[C]. Eighth International Conference on Digital Image Processing(ICDIP), Chengdu, China, 2016: 10033.

Chapter 7

FF-TL: An Effective Tread Pattern Image Classification Algorithm Based on Transfer Learning

7.1 Introduction

Tread patterns are related to actual cases and its source is very special. At present, there are not many researches in the field of tread pattern image classification. Literature survey shows that most scholars use texture features to represent tread pattern images[1-3]. For instance, the authors in [1] proposed a texture feature extraction algorithm named as curvelet domain energy distribution algorithm(CEDA). In this algorithm, curvelet transform is applied on tread pattern image and the mean and variance of each subband are concatenated as texture feature vector of the tread pattern image, which is cyclically shifted till the statistics of the subband with maximum percentage of energy comes to the first position. In [2], an improved Tamura texture feature extraction method was proposed. As a global variable, contrast can well describe the statistical distribution of the brightness in the entire tread image, but cannot reflect the local brightness information of the image.

The proposed method made use of the statistical moments of intensity histogram to extract more information from the image for better description. The authors in [3] proposed to fuse gray level co-occurrence matrix (GLCM) and discrete wavelet decomposition, to enhance the performance of texture feature obtained in discrete wavelet transform. In [4], Yan et al. presented a texture feature extraction method which made use of the rotation-invariant property of Radon transform and the translation-invariant property of DT-CWT (dual tree-complex wavelet transform) to provide rotation and translation-invariant texture features. These features though simple and easy to calculate, are found not as effective as other high-dimensional features such as scale-invariant feature transform (SIFT)[5] and histogram of oriented gradient (HOG)[6]. In [5], to reduce the dimensionality of SIFT while reserving its effectiveness in representing tread pattern images as much as possible, the authors combined wavelet transform with SIFT to obtain the texture features of tread images. The authors in [6] presented a rotation-invariant texture feature based on HOG by making use of texture tendency in tread pattern images.

Existing low-level features of tread pattern images as described above are difficult in representing the semantic information that facilitates human understanding in tread pattern classification, due to the so-called semantic gap. Convolution neural network (CNN) has shown powerful ability to learn image representation. CNNs have achieved good performance in image classification[7]. For example, AlexNet achieves excellent classification accuracy compared with traditional algorithms in ILSVRC[8] and CNN-based methods almost dominate the subsequent ILSVRC[9]. In recent years, deeper neural networks have obtained numerous state-of-the-art results in many computer vision applications, such as ResNet for image recognition[10], dual path networks(DPN)[11]

7.2 Related Work

for image classification and object detection tasks.

However, due to the lack of standard large training dataset, directly applying CNN onto tread pattern image classification may cause overfitting and can not achieve the desired results. Inspired by the idea of transfer learning[12], this chapter proposes to obtain CNN features for tread pattern image based on transfer learning. Moreover, to further improve the performance, the CNN feature obtained is fused with low-level tread pattern image feature as final feature of the tread pattern image. Using the fusion feature to train SVM classifier, our experimental results prove the effectiveness of the proposed method for tread pattern image classification.

This chapter is organized as following: Section 7.2 gives a brief description of deep CNN and transfer learning; Section 7.3 introduces the proposed image classification algorithm based on transfer learning; Section 7.4 provides experimental results and analysis; Section 7.5 concludes this chapter.

7.2 Related Work

7.2.1 Convolutional neural network

Convolutional neural network is a kind of deep neural network with convolutional structure, it uses an end-to-end learning model that bridges the gap between low-level visual features and semantic information by convoluting the features at different levels. The CNN was originally proposed by Fukushima[13]. The first CNN in practical applications was LeNet-5, which was applied for recognition task in Minist handwritten digit dataset[14]. CNN network generally consists of the input layer, the convolutional layers, the pooling layers and the fully-connected(FC) layers. The basic structure of CNN is shown in Fig. 7-1.

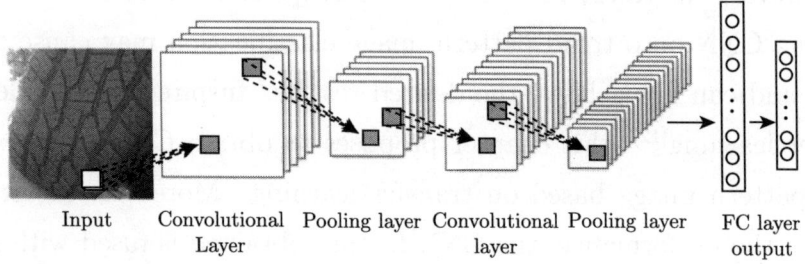

Fig. 7-1 The basic structure of convolution neural network

The convolutional layer, also called feature extraction layer, obtains the robust feature of transform, such as translation, rotation and scaling by convolution operation[15]. The activation function determines the data processing method of the neural network, injects nonlinear factors into the neural network with poor linear expression ability, and enhances the expression ability of the model. The pooling layer, also called the down-sampling layer, by pooling operation, the similar features of the image are aggregated, the dimension of the data is reduced and the adaptability of the network to image changes are enhanced[16]. As example, the classical AlexNet architecture is shown in Fig. 7-2.

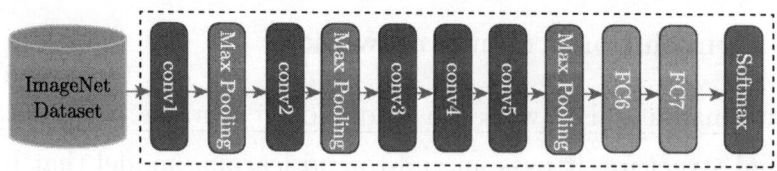

Fig. 7-2 The architecture of AlexNet

7.2.2 Transfer learning

Transfer learning[17,18] refers to the ability to migrate knowledge among tasks by making use of the commonalities between different learning tasks to apply knowledge learned from existing data or environment to new data or environment. The CNNs with transfer learning has achieved great success in the field of image recognition and classification[19,20]. The study shows that CNNs based on transfer learning has achieved significant improvement in the small sample image database[21]. Generally, transfer learning has two steps.

(1) Pre-trained network as feature extractor: A pre-trained network can be used as a feature extractor for any image. For example, one can take a CNN pre-trained model by ImageNet dataset, remove the last classifier layer, then treat the rest as a fixed feature extractor to adapt to a new task. There exist some well pre-trained models on large scale dataset, such as AlexNet model by ImageNet which has been widely used as a feature extractor in transfer learning for various tasks[22].

(2) Fine-tuning the pre-trained model: Fine-tuning is a preferred option to avoid training a CNN from scratch, when the target dataset is not large enough to fully train a new network. The fine-tuning strategy not only retrains the network to adapt to the target dataset, but also includes adjusting the parameters of the network by continuing the back-propagation process. In general, the earlier layers of a CNN learn low level image features, which are applicable to most visual tasks, and the latter layers are high-level features for specific task learning[23]. Therefore, keeping the earlier layers fixed and fine-tuning the last few layers is a good strategy for transfer learning. Fine-tuning avoids the problem of over-fitting due to a lack of training data. It has been shown to be the best strategy for various applications, such as image recognition[24].

7.3 Proposed Algorithm

To reduce the semantic gap, the CNN feature is used to represent tread pattern image. As the tread pattern dataset is small, training CNN from scratch will result in over-fitting. Fortunately, we overcame the training data scarcity problem using transfer learning via fine-tuning to the CNN model. The idea is to transfer the knowledge of a pre-trained CNN model on ImageNet dataset to produce a new model for the task of tread pattern classification. In this chapter, AlexNet architecture is used, considering the hardware facility available.

7.3.1 Fine-tuning the network

Fine-tuning is a process that adapts an already learned model to a new classification model. In order to improve the generalization ability of the neural network for tread pattern images, we set the parameters in the network as follows. In the training procedure based on transfer learning, the feature extractor is initialized as pre-trained AlexNet model on ImageNet only with the last layer removed. After removing the last layer, we adjusted others parameters to fit our tread pattern dataset. First, the last layer in the original model is renamed as 'fc8_new' to make the training continuing. The number of classes is also reset to the number of classes in our tread pattern image dataset. Secondly, 6,500 extra iterations of the CNN are completed using our 5,000 tread pattern images. Then, set the initial base learning rate as 0.001 to fine-tune parameters and the learning rate of 'fc8_new' is enlarged by 10 times to speed up the convergence. Thus, a new CNN model is produced for the task of tread pattern feature extraction.

7.3.2 Feature extraction, feature fusion and SVM classification

Research shows that multi-layer feature fusion can improve the algorithm performance for visual applications[25]. Hence, in the proposed algorithm, the combination of the features from fc6 and fc7 layers are used to provide more accurate representation of tread pattern image. Different weights are applied on fc6 and fc7 features to form a high-level features F_{high},

$$F_{\text{high}} = [\alpha F_{\text{fc6}}, \beta F_{\text{fc7}}] \qquad (7\text{-}1)$$

where experimentally the weights are $\alpha = 0.6$ and $\beta = 0.4$ for fc6 feature F_{fc6} and fc7 feature F_{fc7} respectively. These features usually include noise data and information redundancy. In order to save the algorithm running time and reduce the computational complexity, principal component analysis (PCA) process is applied to reduce the high-level features of dimension 8,192 to dimension 4,096. The feature vector after dimensional reduction is referred to as transfer learning based features(TLF).

Considering both effectiveness and computational complexity, HOG descriptor[26] is used as the low-level features of tread pattern images. In order to better represent tread pattern image, the high-level feature TLF and the low-level feature HOG are fused as the final feature F_{fuse}. Finally, the one-versus-one SVM classifier is trained using for tread pattern image classification.

7.4 Experimental Results

7.4.1 Experimental dataset and performance evaluation parameter

The image classification experiments in this chapter are conducted on the tread pattern image dataset (TPID) from Center for Image and Information Processing (CIIP-TPID) in Xi'an University of Posts and

Telecommunications. It includes 5,000 tread pattern images with 100 classes. Fig. 7-3 shows some samples from CIIP-TPID.

Fig. 7-3 Samples in tread pattern images

The performance evaluation parameter is classification accuracy,

$$\mathrm{CA} = \left(\frac{N}{M}\right) \times 100\% \qquad (7\text{-}2)$$

Where N is the number of samples correctly classified, M is the total number of samples to be classified.

7.4.2 Experimental results and analysis

1. Experiment 1: Comparison of different CNN features

In this experiment, we compare the performance of different CNN features for classification, ① TLF: the proposed transfer learning based features; ② PMF: using pre-trained model as the feature extractor; ③ TSF: using CNN model trained from scratch of TPID. The results are shown in Table 7-1.

The results prove that the proposed TLF achieves best classification accuracy and outperforms other CNN features.

7.4 Experimental Results

Table 7-1 Comparison of different deep learning algorithms

Feature name	Classification accuracy
TLF	79.6%
PMF	61.8%
TSF	65.3%
fc6	71.9%
fc7	73.2%

2. Experiment 2: Low-level feature selection

Different low-level image features are compared for tread pattern image classification capability: ① HOG by Dalal et al.[26]; ② DWT-based texture feature[27]; ③ Curvelet energy distribution algorithm(CEDA)[1]; ④ Tamura-based texture feature[28]; ⑤ SIFT[29]. The results are shown in Fig. 7-4.

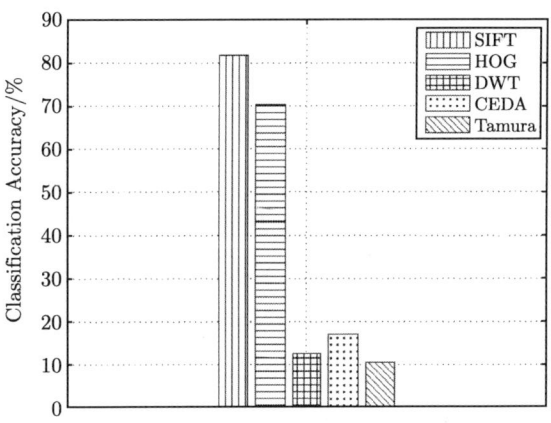

Fig. 7-4 Low-level feature comparison

Though SIFT provides the best classification performance among all the features tested, considering both classification performance and computational complexity, HOG descriptor is selected as the low-level features of tread pattern images and is fused with TLF for tread pattern classification.

3. Experiment 3: Fusion TLF with HOG

In our experiments, we compared the classification performance of the fused features (TLF+HOG) with single feature TLF and HOG. In addition, TSF+HOG was also tested to prove the advantage of TLF.

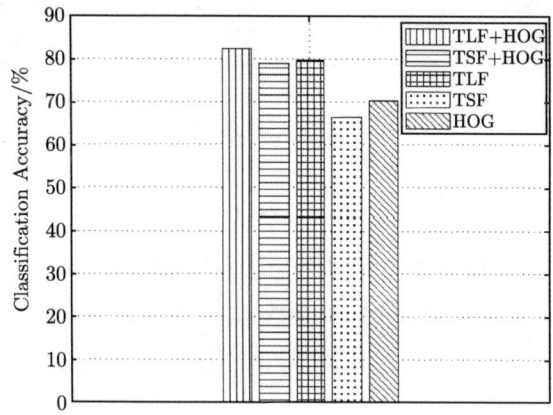

Fig. 7-5 Classification performance of the fusion feature

It can be seen from the above experimental results in Fig. 7-5 that the fusion feature provides higher classification precision than the single features.

The above experimental results prove that ① The proposed CNN features based on transfer learning via fine-tuning (TLF) outperforms all other CNN features. ② Fusion CNN features with conventional low-level image features can further improve the effectiveness of the tread pattern image feature in pattern classification.

7.5 Conclusions

To improve the classification accuracy of tread pattern images, this chapter presented a transfer learning based feature fusion algorithm. The algorithm transfers pre-trained CNN model to tread pattern image database by transfer learning and fine-tuning the model parameters. Then the features in different fully-connected layers fc6 and fc7 layer are extracted and concatenated with different weights as the high-level feature. The high-level features are then combined with low-level image feature as fusion feature to train SVM classifier for more accurate classification. Experimental results prove the effectiveness of the proposed algorithm for tread pattern classification.

References

[1] YAN H, LIM K P. Study on rotation-invariant texture feature extraction for tire pattern retrieval[J]. Multidimensional systems and signal processing, 2017, 28(2): 757-770.

[2] LIU Y, LI Z, GAO Z M. An improved texture feature extraction method for tire tread patterns[C]. Intelligence Science and Big Data Engineering, Berlin Heidelberg, 2013: 705-713.

[3] JIA S Y, MA J T. Tire pattern retrieval based on wavelet transform and gray level co-occurrence matrix[J]. Computer measurement & control, 2016, 24(6): 210-213.

[4] YAN H, LIU Y. An improved texture feature extraction method based on radon transform[C]. IEEE International Symposium on Computational Intelligence and Design, Hangzhou, China, 2015: 481-485.

[5] WANG S, LIU Y, LI D X. An improved SIFT feature extraction method for tire tread patterns retrieval[C]. IEEE International Symposium on Computational Intelligence and Design, Hangzhou, China, 2014: 539-543.

[6] LIU Y, GE Y X, WANG F P. Texture feature extraction based on histogram of oriented gradient domain texture tendency for tire pattern retrieval[C]. IEEE International Conference Intelligent Control and Information Processing, Hangzhou, China, 2017: 1-7.

[7] SUN Y, WANG X, TANG X. Deep learning face representation from predicting 10000 classes[C]. IEEE Conference on Computer Vision and Pattern Recognition, Columbus, USA, 2014: 1891-1898.

[8] KRIZHEVSKY A, SUTSKEVER I, HINTON G E. ImageNet classification with deep convolutional neural networks[J]. Communications of the ACM, 2012, 60(2): 1097-1105.

[9] RUSSAKOVSKY O, DENG J, SU H, et al. ImageNet large scale visual recognition challenge[J]. International journal of computer vision, 2015, 115(3) : 211-252.

[10] HE K, ZHANG X Y, REN S Q. Deep residual learning for image recognition[C]. IEEE Conference on Computer Vision and Pattern Recognition, Las Vegas, USA, 2016: 770-778.

[11] CHEN Y P, LI J N, XIAO H X. Dual Path Networks[J]. Neural information processing systems, 2017, 66: 4467-4475.

[12] OQUAB M, BOTTOU L, LAPTEV I, et al. Learning and transferring mid-level image representations using convolutional neural networks[C]. Computer Vision and Pattern Recognition, Columbus, Ohio, 2014: 1717-1724.

[13] FUKUSHIMA K. Neocognitron: A self-organizing neural network model for a mechanism of pattern recognition unaffected by shift in position[J]. Biological cybernetics, 1980, 36(4): 193-202.

[14] LECUN Y, BOTTOU L, BENGIO M. Gradient-based learning applied to document recognition[J]. Proceedings of the IEEE, 1998, 86(11): 2278-2324.

[15] SZEGEDY C, LIU W, JIA Y. Going deeper with convolution[C]. IEEE Conference on Computer Vision and Pattern Recognition, Boston, USA, 2015: 1-9.

[16] LECUN C, BENGIO Y, HINTON G E. Deep learning[J]. Nature, 2015, 521(7553): 436-444.

[17] PAN S J, YANG Q. A Survey on Transfer Learning[J]. IEEE transactions on knowledge and data engineering, 2010, 22(10): 1345-1359.

[18] BENGIO Y. Deep learning of representations for unsupervised and transfer learning[C]. Workshop on Unsupervised & Transfer Learning, Washington, USA, 2012: 1-20.

[19] CARVAJAL V A, ROMERO D G, SAPPA A D. Fine-tuning based deep convolutional networks for lepidopterous genus recognition[C]. Ibero-American Congress on Pattern Recognition, Lima, Peru, 2016: 467-475.

[20] XIE M, JEAN N, BURKE M. Transfer learning from deep features for remote sensing and poverty mapping[C]. The AAAI Conference on Artificial Intelligence, New Orleans, USA, 2016: 3929-3935.

[21] ZEILER M D, FERGUS R. Visualizing and understanding convolutional networks[C]. European Conference on Computer Vision, Columbus, Ohio, 2014: 818-833.

[22] KRIZHEVSKY A, SUTSKEVER I, HINTON G E. ImageNet classification with deep convolutional newral networks[J]. Communications of ACM, 2017, 60(6): 84-90.

[23] TAJBAKHSH N, SHIN J Y, GURUDU S R. Convolutional neural networks for medical image analysis: full training or fine tuning[J]. IEEE transactions on medical imaging, 2016, 35(5): 1299-1312.

[24] LIMA E, SUN X, DONG J. Learning and transferring convolutional neural network knowledge to ocean front recognition[J]. IEEE geoscience and remote sensing letters, 2017, 14(3): 354-358.

[25] KULKA P, ZEPEDA J, JURIE F. Hybrid multi-layer deep CNN/ aggregator feature for image classification[C]. IEEE International Conference on Acoustics, Speech and Signal Processing, Queensland, Australia, 2015: 1379-1383.

[26] DALAL N, TRIGGS B. Histograms of oriented gradients for human detection[C]. Computer Vision and Pattern Recognition, San Diego, CA, USA, 2005: 886-893.

[27] HEIL C E, WALNUT A F. Continuous and discrete wavelet transforms[J]. Siam review, 1989, 31(4): 628-666.

[28] TAMURA H, MORI S, YAMAWAKI M. Textural features corresponding to visual perception[J]. IEEE transactions on systems man & cybernetics, 1978, 8(6): 460-473.

[29] LOWE D G. Distinctive image features from scale-invariant key-points[J]. International journal of computer vision, 2004, 60(2): 91-110.

Chapter 8

Summary and Future Work

8.1 Summary of the Book

Tire pattern image retrieval (TPIR) is an important research area in both commercial and forensic applications. Although content-based image retrieval (CBIR) has been studied for decades, little has been done for tire pattern retrieval due to the lack of such data in the past. The research outcome in TPIR and its application in practical application scenario is still far from user's expectations due to the lack of standard test bed and the fact that only a small number of researchers are working in this field.

The aim of this book is two-folded. The first is to provide a comprehensive survey on the research outcome in TPIR, so that researchers can easily understand what has been achieved in this field and what are still needed to be done. The second is to discuss how to design TPIR system by presenting a few different algorithms we proposed, so that researchers in this field can compare different types of methods and understand their different performance in TPIR.

Different aspects of the research in TPIR are covered in this book, including tire pattern image datasets, performance evaluations, low-level tire pattern feature extraction and high-level semantic learning.

According to the application scenarios, four major categories of the state-of-the-art techniques in tire pattern retrieval are found including tire tread pattern retrieval, tread surface wear feature extraction, video tread pattern retrieval and tire indentation mark retrieval.

Texture feature extraction can be done in space domain or transform domain. This books describes and compares texture features obtained in different domains, for example, the modified Tamura feature in Chapter 3 and the HOG-TT texture feature in Chapter 6 are all in space domain, the Radon-DTCWT algorithm and the CEDA algorithm in Chapter 5 are in transform domain, while the H-SIFT feature presented in Chapter 4 combines image transformation and space domain feature extraction. Experimental results demonstrate that transform domain based methods are more effective in describing tire patterns.

It is observed most existing algorithms are based on combination or modification of traditional texture features without considering the intrinsic characteristics of tire pattern images. With the intention to address this problem, the algorithms in Chapter 5 and Chapter 6 are designed. Different rotation and direction of tire patterns are often encountered and is insufficient to use the conventional multi-scale texture feature extraction method which is not rotational invariant. To alleviate this problem, Chapter 5 proposed two new texture feature extraction methods based on the Radon transform and curvelet transform. In Chapter 6, a HOG-based texture feature extraction algorithm is specially designed for tire pattern image description.

Deep learning as a hot research topic which has been proved to be powerful in image classification and retrieval tasks, has first time been explored for TPIR. Convolutional neural network(CNN) is a kind of deep neural network with convolutional structure. It uses an end-to-end learning model that bridges the gap between low-level visual features and semantic information by convoluting the features at different levels. To relieve the over-fitting problem due to the lack of large training dataset of tire pattern images in model training, Chapter 7 presented an algorithm based on transfer learning. It transfers the knowledge of the pre-trained CNN model on large scale ImageNet dataset to the task of tire pattern classification. The model parameters are fine-tuned through back-propagation using tire pattern image data. The features from the last two fully-connected layers are combined as the CNN feature. For more effective representation of tire pattern images, the features from the CNN model are combined with HOG as fusion feature, which is used to train SVM classifier for tire pattern image classification. Experimental results demonstrated the outstanding performance of the proposed algorithm. This tells that introducing CNN in TPIR is beneficial and deserves further exploration with large-scale tire pattern image database.

8.2 Discussion of Future Work

From our study and findings in this research, also taking into account the demand from practical applications, the following issues need substantial effort to be explored further.

It has been found that a standard database is yet to be created to include large variety of tire patterns for the research experiment and evaluation. There also needs a systematic evaluation on existing techniques and approaches on tire pattern image retrieval. Although texture features have been predominantly used in existing approaches, other techniques such as color and shape features should also be investigated.

In practical application scenario, there are cases that only tire indentation mark image is available without any information on tire tread.

The connection between tire tread pattern image and tire indentation marks is an interesting research topic of important practical value. As tire indentation information varies with the indentation carriers such as land, snow, etc., this task is challenging. Deep learning could be a potential tool in learning this relationship on the condition that large scale training set is available.

8.3 Acknowledgment

The work in this book was supported by National Natural Science Foundation of China project (No. 61202183), Fund project of Shaanxi Province Education Office (No.12JK0504), Science and Technology Project Fund (No.2016GABJC51) under Ministry of Public Security of China, and National Natural Science Fund of China (No.61671377).

Appendix 1: CIIP Tread Indentation Database

Tire tread pattern image database and the corresponding tire indentation mark database are 720 images, 12 classes. Each class contains 10 tire tread pattern images and 50 tire indentation mark images.

The sample images are shown below.

Appendix 2: CIIP Tread Pattern Database

Tire pattern image database with 5,100 images, 102 classes. These images are taken under different light conditions, with different scale and angle.

The sample images are shown below.

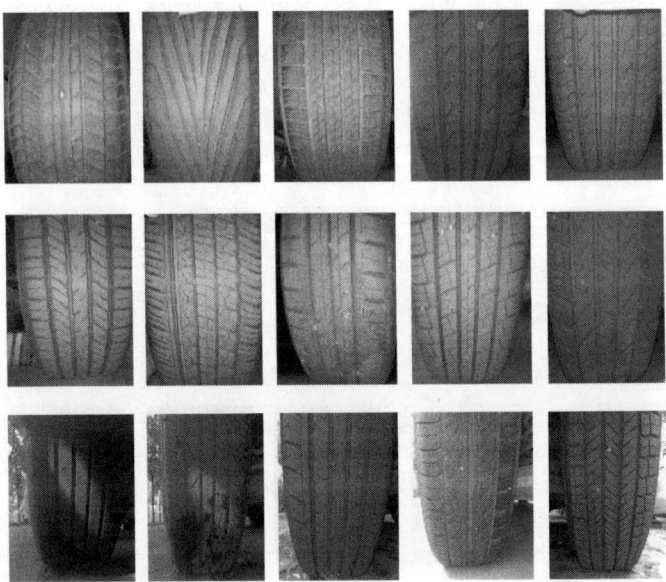